Pathfinder

Exploring Career and Educational Paths

Fourth Edition

Norene Lindsay

JIST
Works
America's Career Publisher®

Pathfinder, Fourth Edition
Exploring Career and Educational Paths

© 2010 by Norene Lindsay and Sherry Brown

Published by JIST Works, an imprint of JIST Publishing
875 Montreal Way
St. Paul, MN 55102

Phone: 800-648-JIST   E-mail: info@jist.com   Web site: www.jist.com

Note to instructors. This book has substantial support materials, including the *Pathfinder Teacher's Guide CD-ROM,* Fourth Edition (ISBN: 978-1-59357-748-3), which includes PowerPoint slides; the *Individual Career Portfolio,* Fourth Edition (ISBN: 978-1-59357-774-2), and videos. Call 800-648-JIST or visit www.jist.com for details.

About career materials published by JIST. Our materials encourage people to be self-directed and to take control of their destinies. We work hard to provide excellent content, solid advice, and techniques that get results. If you have questions about this book or other JIST products, call 800-648-JIST or visit www.jist.com.

Quantity discounts are available for JIST products. Call 800-648-JIST or visit www.jist.com for a free catalog and more information.

Visit www.jist.com. Find out about our products, get free tables of contents and sample pages, order a catalog, and link to other career-related sites. You can also learn more about JIST authors and JIST training available to professionals.

Workbook Product Manager: Lori Cates Hand
Development Editors: Dave Anderson, Heather Stith
Cover Designer and Interior Layout: Aleata Halbig
Proofreader: Jeanne Clark

Printed in the United States of America

15 14 13 12 11   9 8 7 6 5 4 3

ISBN 978-1-59357-747-6

Contents

PART 4
Postsecondary Educational Paths
Choosing the Right Path for You **71**

PART 5
Career Research
Matching Career Interests and Educational Choices with Jobs **83**

PART 6
Plans for the Future
Keeping Records **111**

PART 1

Career Paths

Exploring Career Interest Groups

A large part of your adult life—about 45 years—will be spent working. Spending time now to explore the kind of work that you would enjoy and be good at makes sense.

Part 1 begins your journey as a pathfinder, taking you into a new world of career exploration. You will be introduced to the many possible career paths you might choose. You'll learn about careers you know, such as a firefighter, nurse, or salesperson, and careers that you may never have heard about, such as a desktop publisher, microbiologist, or numerical control machine tool operator.

With thousands of possible career paths open to you, your choices should be well informed: based on knowledge about careers, yourself, and your interests. This part of Pathfinder *will help you gain that knowledge. To begin, you'll be asked to take a career interest assessment. To learn what an assessment is and how it will help you, turn to the next page.*

Take a Career Interest Assessment

To help discover career paths you might like, *Pathfinder* begins with a career interest assessment. It may sound like a test, but don't let the title fool you. An assessment is NOT a test. It is a tool that helps you discover what you like. Any answer you give is a "right" answer because an assessment helps you discover what's right for you.

To take the assessment, you will read short statements. Then you will check the items that describe you and your interests. You'll be asked to make choices in the following areas:

▼ Work activities that seem interesting to you

▼ Personal qualities that describe you

▼ Free-time activities you do now or might like to do

▼ School subjects or activities that you do well in or enjoy

An assessment is the first step to discovering careers that you might like and an exciting step forward on your career path. To take this first step, just read the directions.

Directions

The Career Interest Assessment is divided into 16 groups. Each group relates to 16 major career interest areas. In each area, you will check what interests you in work activities, personal qualities, free-time activities, and school subjects. You do not need to do all 16 groups at once. Doing different groups at different times will not affect the results. Your teacher will help you decide how many groups to do at one time.

As you complete the assessment, follow these guidelines:

▼ Each group has short statements in four areas. Simply follow the directions for each area. Do not spend much time thinking about your answer. Just read the statement and respond to it. Your first thought is generally the best.

▼ The same or similar statements will appear in more than one group. Don't worry about how you answered it before. Just read the statement and respond to it.

▼ You may be asked about school subjects you have not taken yet or things that don't apply to you. Just leave these items blank.

Remember, there are only right answers! You are the only one who knows if an item matches your feelings, personality, and preferences.

Group 1

Check the Work Activities That Interest You:

_____ Managing a beef or dairy ranch
_____ Planning how to sell farm crops or animals
_____ Hiring and directing workers who plant crops or raise livestock
_____ Choosing and buying chemicals to prevent plant diseases
_____ Maintaining trails and facilities at national parks
_____ Drilling for oil on an offshore platform
_____ Raising fish in a hatchery
_____ Running a greenhouse
_____ Managing how forests are used
_____ Planting and taking care of lawns and landscapes using power equipment
_____ Operating farm machinery such as tractors
_____ Directing a logging crew
_____ Educating people about the need for conservation
_____ Diagnosing and treating sick animals
_____ Developing methods to grow better crops

Check the Sentences That Describe You:

_____ I like to decide things for myself.
_____ I like to plan my own work.
_____ I like to work and play outside.
_____ I like to be busy all the time.
_____ I like to work alone.

Check the Free-Time Activities You Do Now or Might Like to Do:

_____ Belong to a 4-H Club
_____ Grow vegetables in a garden
_____ Feed, exercise, and clean up after animals
_____ Design and plant a flower garden
_____ Lead a scouting or outdoor group
_____ Belong to an environmental club
_____ Camp, hike, and fish
_____ Mow the lawn
_____ Read farm animal or wildlife magazines
_____ Drive a tractor on a family farm
_____ Study plants in parks or forests
_____ Groom pets and other animals
_____ Take care of sick pets
_____ Trim bushes and trees
_____ Go horseback riding

Check the School Subjects or Activities That You Do Well in or Enjoy:

_____ Agriculture
_____ Animal Science
_____ Environmental Science
_____ Chemistry
_____ Mathematics
_____ Science
_____ Biology
_____ Physical Education

Group 2

Check the Work Activities That Interest You:

_____ Supervising workers on a construction site to make sure the building project matches plans

_____ Training workers to operate equipment

_____ Installing a new roof on a house or building

_____ Building or making repairs underwater using scuba gear or a diving suit

_____ Installing windows using hand and power tools

_____ Loading and unloading trucks to provide materials and equipment for other workers

_____ Checking and repairing wiring and equipment using hand and power tools

_____ Measuring and marking floors to be tiled following blueprints

_____ Repairing or building boats

_____ Painting the inside or outside of homes and buildings

_____ Operating a bulldozer at a construction site

_____ Using computers to prepare blueprints for buildings, bridges, and other structures

_____ Inspecting a construction site to make sure safety regulations are followed

_____ Installing the plumbing in a new house

_____ Mixing concrete using a portable mixer

Check the Sentences That Describe You:

_____ I like to give directions and instructions to other people.

_____ I like to make my own decisions.

_____ I like to plan my own work.

_____ I like to work by myself.

_____ I like to be busy all the time.

Check the Free-Time Activities You Do Now or Might Like to Do:

_____ Build stage sets for a school or community play

_____ Sketch machines

_____ Paint rooms, fences, or houses

_____ Fix faucets and toilets

_____ Make furniture or cabinets

_____ Build model airplanes, cars, or boats

_____ Lead a club or group

_____ Volunteer to build houses for the needy

_____ Mow the lawn

_____ Set up and operate a model train

_____ Do electrical wiring

_____ Design an addition for your home

_____ Read mechanical or automotive magazines

_____ Draw posters for an organization or political campaign

_____ Refinish furniture

Check the School Subjects or Activities That You Do Well in or Enjoy:

_____ Art

_____ Mathematics

_____ Chemistry

_____ Carpentry

_____ Algebra

_____ Geometry

_____ Industrial or Technology Education

_____ Science

Group 3

Check the Work Activities That Interest You:

_____ Reading and correcting writers' stories or articles

_____ Painting or drawing pictures

_____ Designing and building scenery for plays

_____ Taking photographs or shooting videos to illustrate a story

_____ Reading items written in a foreign language and rewriting them into English

_____ Announcing on radio or television programs

_____ Writing instructions on how to put something together

_____ Designing and planning flower arrangements for special occasions such as a wedding

_____ Writing stories, poems, books, or newspaper or magazine articles

_____ Designing clothes and cutting patterns to make them

_____ Using a computer to create magazine artwork

_____ Acting in a play, television show, or movie

_____ Operating a camera to shoot films

_____ Playing a musical instrument or singing in a band or orchestra

Check the Sentences That Describe You:

_____ I like to plan my own work.

_____ I like to see results from the work I do.

_____ I like to use my abilities.

_____ I like to make my own decisions.

_____ I like to try out my own ideas.

Check the Free-Time Activities You Do Now or Might Like to Do:

_____ Design things on a computer

_____ Work on a school yearbook or newspaper

_____ Act in a play or perform in a talent show

_____ Build stage sets for a school or community play

_____ Paint pictures

_____ Sculpt things from clay

_____ Do arts and crafts projects

_____ Create hairstyles for friends

_____ Write stories, plays, or articles

_____ Sing in a choir or other group

_____ Take photographs or shoot videos of friends and family

_____ Play a musical instrument

_____ Illustrate a book or magazine

_____ Write and draw a cartoon

_____ Modify photographs using computer software

Check the School Subjects or Activities That You Do Well in or Enjoy:

_____ English

_____ Drama or Dance

_____ Art

_____ Band or Orchestra

_____ Choir or Chorus

_____ Creative Writing

_____ Foreign Language

_____ Computer Design

Group 4

Check the Work Activities That Interest You:

_____ Transferring or firing employees based on their work performance

_____ Analyzing employee needs to develop new training programs

_____ Setting goals and deadlines for a department of a business or organization

_____ Answering the telephone, giving information to callers, taking information, and transferring calls to others

_____ Planning work activities and preparing work schedules

_____ Devising, putting into action, and interpreting rules and policies

_____ Recruiting, interviewing, and selecting qualified job applicants

_____ Keeping business files in order

_____ Coordinating the activities of multiple departments of a business or organization

_____ Negotiating contracts with clients, customers, and service providers

_____ Recording details of calls, dispatches, and messages and keeping logs and files using a computer

_____ Preparing and maintaining employee records

_____ Processing legal documents and papers

_____ Compiling payroll data from timesheets and other records

_____ Sorting and verifying the accuracy of data using a computer database

Check the Sentences That Describe You:

_____ I like to give directions or instructions to others.

_____ I like to plan my own work.

_____ I like to be busy all the time.

_____ I like to work alone.

_____ I want to be treated fairly.

Check the Free-Time Activities You Do Now or Might Like to Do:

_____ Be the president or treasurer of a club or group

_____ Collect stamps or coins

_____ Create an online newsletter for a school group

_____ Read business magazines and newspapers

_____ Balance checkbooks for family members

_____ Keep score for an athletic event

_____ Help in the school library

_____ Conduct house-to-house or telephone surveys for a school group

_____ Compete in debates or speech meets

_____ Operate a CB or ham radio

_____ Speak on radio or television

_____ Recruit members for a club or organization

_____ Raise money for a charity

_____ Write for a school newspaper

_____ Create mailing labels for a group or organization

Check the School Subjects or Activities That You Do Well in or Enjoy:

_____ English

_____ Computers

_____ Accounting

_____ Keyboarding

_____ Writing

_____ Mathematics

_____ Speech

_____ Business

Group 5

Check the Work Activities That Interest You:

_____ Advising teachers in planning classes and managing student behavior

_____ Talking with park staff to decide what programs to present to the public

_____ Developing instructional materials to be used by educators

_____ Preparing artifacts for exhibition in a museum

_____ Supervising peer tutoring programs

_____ Officiating at sporting events, games, or competitions

_____ Competing in athletic events and competitive sports

_____ Planning physical education programs and activities

_____ Coaching athletes in a specific sport

_____ Creating and helping manage fitness plans for individuals

_____ Developing distance learning training courses

_____ Instructing students using lectures, discussions, and demonstrations

_____ Maintaining student records

_____ Advising students on courses to help them plan their programs of study

_____ Developing and giving tests

_____ Grading tests and papers

_____ Instructing library patrons on how to find resources and information

_____ Organizing books, magazines, DVDs, and other publications in a library

Check the Sentences That Describe You:

_____ I like to give directions and instructions to other people.

_____ I like to plan my own work.

_____ I like to see results from my work.

_____ I like to do things for other people.

_____ I like to make my own decisions.

Check the Free-Time Activities You Do Now or Might Like to Do:

_____ Go camping or hiking

_____ Help family members with homework

_____ Plan or arrange school or community programs

_____ Lead a club or group

_____ Teach games to children as a volunteer at a preschool

_____ Babysit

_____ Help people who have disabilities take walks

_____ Join the debate club or do public speaking

_____ Volunteer as a counselor at a youth camp or community center

_____ Teach in a religious school

_____ Coach children in sports

_____ Research things that interest you

_____ Tutor younger students

_____ Help in the school library

_____ Help non-native speakers learn English

Check the School Subjects or Activities That You Do Well in or Enjoy:

_____ Mathematics

_____ English

_____ Science

_____ Social Studies

_____ Writing

_____ Foreign Language

_____ Psychology

_____ Computers

Group 6

Check the Work Activities That Interest You:

_____ Analyzing financial risks to see how they would affect a company's business

_____ Directing the part of a company that provides financial services

_____ Examining, evaluating, and processing loan applications

_____ Overseeing the flow of cash for a business or organization

_____ Inspecting property in order to determine its current value

_____ Planning a budget for a business or a department

_____ Determining the creditworthiness of customers

_____ Helping bank customers complete transactions

_____ Settling claims for property or crop damage

_____ Notifying customers of delinquent accounts

_____ Collecting information on what customers like and their buying habits

_____ Customizing insurance programs to suit individual customers

_____ Deciding when to buy or sell stocks and bonds

_____ Keeping records of business transactions

_____ Preparing and filing annual tax returns for businesses

Check the Sentences That Describe You:

_____ I like to give instructions or directions to others.

_____ I like to plan my own work.

_____ I like to make my own decisions.

_____ I like to work in a safe and comfortable environment.

_____ I want to be treated fairly.

Check the Free-Time Activities You Do Now or Might Like to Do:

_____ Balance checkbooks for family members

_____ Compare costs on something you want to buy

_____ Budget your own money

_____ Help run a school or community fair or carnival

_____ Plan and arrange school programs

_____ Read business magazines

_____ Lead a group

_____ Serve as the president of a club

_____ Read newspapers

_____ Join the debate club or do public speaking

_____ Be the announcer at a school event

_____ Serve as the treasurer of a club or group

_____ Organize volunteers for a school program

_____ Buy large quantities of food for a school event

_____ Conduct house-to-house or telephone surveys for a cause

Check the School Subjects or Activities That You Do Well in or Enjoy:

_____ English

_____ Writing

_____ Speech

_____ Mathematics

_____ Accounting

_____ Business

_____ Advanced Mathematics

_____ Computers

Group 7

Check the Work Activities That Interest You:

_____ Reviewing and analyzing legislation and public policy and recommending changes

_____ Speaking to community groups to explain programs and policies

_____ Conducting investigations to resolve complaints and violations of laws

_____ Preparing budgets and monitoring expenditures

_____ Conducting interviews, surveys, and inspections concerning land usage

_____ Holding meetings with special interest groups and the public to discuss community plans

_____ Preparing reports using statistics, charts, and graphs

_____ Collecting air, water, and gas samples for testing purposes

_____ Inspecting crops and livestock

_____ Investigating equal opportunity complaints and settling disputes

_____ Examining immigration applications, visas, and passports to determine admission, residence, and travel eligibility

_____ Directing crews working on fire lines during forest fires

_____ Inspecting buildings to ensure they meet safety requirements

_____ Planning and directing the storage and maintenance of public records

_____ Responding to requests for information from the public and government officials

Check the Sentences That Describe You:

_____ I like to give instructions or directions to others.

_____ I like to be busy all the time.

_____ I like to plan my own work.

_____ I want to have steady employment.

_____ I want to be treated fairly.

Check the Free-Time Activities You Do Now or Might Like to Do:

_____ Help run a school or community fair or carnival

_____ Serve as the president of a club

_____ Serve as a volunteer interviewer in a social service organization

_____ Plan and arrange school programs

_____ Read detective stories or watch detective shows

_____ Write letters and e-mail messages to friends and family

_____ Serve as a secretary of a club or other organization

_____ Read newspapers

_____ Join the debate club or do public speaking

_____ Collect rocks or minerals

_____ Campaign for political candidates or issues

_____ Organize volunteers for a school program

_____ Buy large quantities of food for a school event

_____ Belong to an environmental club

_____ Conduct house-to-house or telephone surveys for a cause

Check the School Subjects or Activities That You Do Well in or Enjoy:

_____ English	_____ Business
_____ Writing	_____ Sociology
_____ Speech	_____ Computers
_____ Mathematics	
_____ Government	

Group 8

Check the Work Activities That Interest You:

_____ Directing investigations into the cause of a death

_____ Helping a pharmacist prepare and give out medicine

_____ Operating on patients to fix problems, repair injuries, or prevent disease

_____ Cleaning teeth using dental instruments

_____ Exposing and developing X-ray film of teeth

_____ Examining eyes to test vision and look for any diseases

_____ Treating foot problems such as corns, calluses, tumors, and cysts using surgical methods

_____ Conducting chemical analyses of body fluids to see whether they are normal

_____ Drawing blood from patients

_____ Diagnosing and treating sick animals

_____ Designing and building special equipment such as splints and braces

_____ Administering medication as directed by a doctor or nurse

_____ Measuring and recording a patient's vital signs such as heart rate and blood pressure

_____ Evaluating the physical condition of athletes and giving them exercises to strengthen muscles

_____ Investigating complaints about violations of public health laws or bad products or services

Check the Sentences That Describe You:

_____ I like to do things for other people.

_____ I like to see the results of my work.

_____ I like to use my abilities.

_____ I like to plan my own work.

_____ I want to work with friendly people.

Check the Free-Time Activities You Do Now or Might Like to Do:

_____ Apply first aid in emergencies

_____ Volunteer for the Red Cross

_____ Read medical magazines

_____ Serve as a volunteer aide in a hospital, nursing home, or retirement home

_____ Advise family members on their personal problems

_____ Help take care of sick or old relatives and friends

_____ Help lead physical exercises for people who have disabilities

_____ Experiment with a chemistry set

_____ Perform experiments for a science fair

_____ Help people who have disabilities take walks

_____ Serve as a volunteer in a fire department or emergency rescue squad

_____ Read scientific magazines

_____ Take care of sick pets

_____ Join the debate club or do public speaking

_____ Help persuade others to sign a petition

Check the School Subjects or Activities That You Do Well in or Enjoy:

_____ Science

_____ Mathematics

_____ Biology

_____ English

_____ Chemistry

_____ Computers

_____ Psychology

_____ Health

Group 9

Check the Work Activities That Interest You:

_____ Greeting and registering guests at a hotel or motel

_____ Interviewing and hiring workers and scheduling their duties and work shifts

_____ Selecting and purchasing new furniture for hotel rooms and lobbies

_____ Explaining hunting and fishing laws to groups

_____ Planning a guided tour for a group of travelers

_____ Giving out and collecting passenger boarding passes and tickets

_____ Transporting customers and baggage using a motor vehicle

_____ Providing services and instructions to passengers during an airplane flight

_____ Applying nail polish to a customer's nails

_____ Cutting, coloring, and styling a customer's hair

_____ Baking breads, rolls, cakes, and pastries to sell

_____ Sewing clothes to fit a customer's measurements

_____ Taking orders and serving food in a restaurant

Check the Sentences That Describe You:

_____ I like to give directions and instructions to others.

_____ I like to plan my own work.

_____ I like to make my own decisions.

_____ I like to do things for other people.

_____ I want to work with friendly people.

Check the Free-Time Activities You Do Now or Might Like to Do:

_____ Plan family recreational activities

_____ Set the table and serve family meals

_____ Lead a group

_____ Usher for school or community events

_____ Do the announcing or be an emcee for a program

_____ Be a counselor at a camp or community center

_____ Help run a school carnival

_____ Coach children or youth in sports activities

_____ Set tables for a club or school function

_____ Create hairstyles for friends

_____ Apply make-up for a school play

_____ Bake and decorate cakes

_____ Babysit

_____ Plan and cook meals

_____ Play baseball, basketball, football, or other sports

Check the School Subjects or Activities That You Do Well in or Enjoy:

_____ Mathematics

_____ Family and Consumer Sciences

_____ English

_____ Speech

_____ Writing

_____ Business

_____ Accounting

_____ Physical Education

Group 10

Check the Work Activities That Interest You:

_____ Developing rehabilitation programs for offenders and inmates

_____ Counseling students in handling issues such as family, financial, and educational problems

_____ Planning and conducting programs to prevent substance abuse

_____ Investigating child abuse or neglect cases

_____ Counseling individuals and groups concerning their spiritual, emotional, and personal needs

_____ Organizing and leading religious services

_____ Scheduling special events such as camps, conferences, seminars, and retreats

_____ Visiting people in hospitals and prisons to provide them with comfort and support

_____ Caring for children in a group home, nursery school, or day-care center

_____ Organizing and participating in recreational activities

_____ Reading to children and teaching them how to paint, draw, make crafts, and sing songs

_____ Providing care for people who are unable to care for themselves

_____ Assisting individuals in filling out applications, questionnaires, and other forms

_____ Selecting and referring applicants to public assistance or public housing agencies

Check the Sentences That Describe You:

_____ I like to get a feeling of accomplishment from the work I do.

_____ I like to plan my own work.

_____ I like to give directions and instructions to other people.

_____ I like to do things for other people.

_____ I want to have steady employment.

Check the Free-Time Activities You Do Now or Might Like to Do:

_____ Plan family recreational activities

_____ Listen to friends and help them with personal problems

_____ Volunteer in a hospital, nursing home, or retirement home

_____ Help people with disabilities take walks

_____ Lead a group

_____ Serve as a volunteer counselor at a camp or community center

_____ Volunteer at a religious organization

_____ Teach in a religious school

_____ Teach games to children

_____ Plan and cook meals

_____ Help organize things at home

_____ Coach children or youth in sports activities

_____ Babysit

_____ Help take care of sick or old relatives and friends

_____ Plan or arrange school and community programs

Check the School Subjects or Activities That You Do Well in or Enjoy:

_____	Psychology	_____	Child Development
_____	Family and Consumer Sciences	_____	Philosophy
_____	English	_____	Religion
_____	Speech	_____	Social Work

Group 11

Check the Work Activities That Interest You:

_____ Recruiting, hiring, training, and supervising computer support staff

_____ Reviewing project plans in order to coordinate activity and control costs

_____ Designing computer systems to meet information processing needs

_____ Assisting computer users with problems

_____ Installing computer software and hardware

_____ Developing software and systems to protect computer files against security threats

_____ Designing and implementing network configurations and architecture

_____ Assembling and installing machines according to specifications

_____ Testing electronic components and circuits to locate defects

_____ Designing, developing, and modifying software systems

_____ Evaluating software or hardware and recommending improvements

_____ Modifying existing databases and database management systems

_____ Writing, updating, and maintaining computer programs or software programs to handle specific jobs

_____ Troubleshooting computer software and hardware systems and implementing solutions

Check the Sentences That Describe You:

_____ I want to be paid well compared to other workers.

_____ I like to plan my own work.

_____ I like to try out my own ideas.

_____ I like to use my abilities.

_____ I want to work in a safe and comfortable environment.

Check the Free-Time Activities You Do Now or Might Like to Do:

_____ Write computer programs

_____ Belong to a computer club

_____ Serve as the president of a club

_____ Play chess

_____ Solve complex puzzles

_____ Create and manage Web pages

_____ Upgrade hardware in personal computers

_____ Take apart or fix mechanical and electronic devices

_____ Assemble radios, computers, and other devices from kits

_____ Play computer or video games

_____ Read computer magazines

_____ Draw sketches of machines or other mechanical equipment

_____ Read about technological developments such as computers or space travel

_____ Design things on a computer

_____ Repair electrical household appliances

Check the School Subjects or Activities That You Do Well in or Enjoy:

_____ Computers

_____ Mathematics

_____ English

_____ Science

_____ Advanced Mathematics

_____ Keyboarding

_____ Industrial or Technology Education

_____ Algebra

Group 12

Check the Work Activities That Interest You:

_____ Directing the activities of a police force or fire department

_____ Inspecting buildings to see whether they meet fire and safety rules

_____ Investigating, collecting evidence against, and arresting people who are suspected of committing a crime

_____ Driving and guarding armored cars to prevent theft

_____ Serving in the military to keep peace and protect our country

_____ Working as a lawyer to defend a client

_____ Warning or arresting people who break fishing and hunting laws

_____ Assisting a lawyer by interviewing clients and witnesses

_____ Working as a police officer, firefighter, or government agent

_____ Listening to arguments on both sides of an issue and helping people compromise

_____ Photographing crime or accident scenes

_____ Working as a store detective or security guard

_____ Giving first aid to people at accident scenes and taking them to the hospital

_____ Patrolling an international border to prevent people or goods from illegal entry

_____ Patrolling forests and parks to protect people and animals

Check the Sentences That Describe You:

_____ I like to give directions and instructions to others.

_____ I like to see the results of the work I do.

_____ I like to work on my own.

_____ I want to be treated fairly.

_____ I want to work with friendly people.

Check the Free-Time Activities You Do Now or Might Like to Do:

_____ Be a member of the school safety patrol

_____ Be a counselor at a camp

_____ Serve as the president of a club

_____ Learn how to help people in an emergency

_____ Read detective or lawyer stories or watch detective or lawyer shows on television

_____ Play games where you solve a mystery

_____ Hunt or shoot targets

_____ Watch television shows or movies about the military

_____ Teach children safety rules

_____ Volunteer at a hospital

_____ Join the debate club or do public speaking

_____ Learn about self-defense

_____ Listen to family and friends' problems and offer help

_____ Watch television shows about real crimes

_____ Use the Internet or library to research things that interest you

Check the School Subjects or Activities That You Do Well in or Enjoy:

_____ Government	_____ Psychology
_____ Science	_____ Social Studies
_____ History	_____ Physical Education
_____ English	_____ First Aid

Group 13

Check the Work Activities That Interest You:

_____ Assigning workers to tasks such as servicing appliances, checking and repairing cars, or installing machinery

_____ Examining tools and equipment in a work area to make sure they are safe

_____ Connecting electrical wiring to control panels and electric motors

_____ Repairing medical equipment such as CAT scanners and X-ray machines

_____ Keeping airplanes in top mechanical condition

_____ Inspecting products for defects

_____ Using welding equipment to make repairs on ships

_____ Assembling a piece of wooden furniture

_____ Installing and repairing furnaces and air conditioning units

_____ Altering garments such as pants or dresses

_____ Performing check-ups on cars, trucks, or motorcycles and replacing parts or repairing engines

_____ Repairing or tuning musical instruments such as keyboards, guitars, saxophones, or drums

_____ Putting together or taking apart machinery or equipment using hand and power tools

_____ Cleaning, lubricating, and programming machines on an assembly line

_____ Painting cars and trucks

Check the Sentences That Describe You:

_____ I like to give directions or instructions to other people.

_____ I like to plan my own work.

_____ I like to be busy all the time.

_____ I like to make my own decisions.

_____ I like to use machines.

Check the Free-Time Activities You Do Now or Might Like to Do:

_____ Be the leader of a group

_____ Build model airplanes, boats, or cars

_____ Assemble radios, computers, or robots from kits

_____ Operate a ham or CB radio

_____ Fix bicycles

_____ Build or repair radios or televisions

_____ Install home sound equipment

_____ Make sketches of machines or mechanical equipment

_____ Set up and operate model trains

_____ Build stage sets for school or community plays

_____ Repair the family car

_____ Read about technological developments such as computers or space travel

_____ Cook large quantities of food for a party or school function

_____ Repair electrical household appliances

_____ Read car design, mechanical, or boating magazines

Check the School Subjects or Activities That You Do Well in or Enjoy:

_____ Chemistry

_____ Mathematics

_____ Algebra

_____ Physics

_____ Science

_____ Computers

_____ Industrial or Technology Education

_____ Geometry

Group 14

Check the Work Activities That Interest You:

_____ Planning and preparing advertisements to sell products

_____ Supervising and training salespeople

_____ Discussing the terms of sales and service with a customer

_____ Selling computers to businesses and organizations

_____ Taking orders from customers in person, on the phone, or from a Web site

_____ Planning and sketching layouts to meet customers' needs

_____ Putting together product displays in a store to attract customers

_____ Figuring out the sales price of merchandise

_____ Estimating delivery dates and arranging delivery schedules

_____ Renting merchandise to customers

_____ Taking inventory of stock

_____ Demonstrating the use of a product to customers

_____ Keeping records of customers and their orders

_____ Contacting people to convince them to become members of an organization

_____ Doing research to figure out the best ways to sell a product or service

Check the Sentences That Describe You:

_____ I like to give directions or instructions to others.

_____ I like to try out my own ideas.

_____ I like to plan my own work.

_____ I like to see the results of my work.

_____ I like to work alone.

Check the Free-Time Activities You Do Now or Might Like to Do:

_____ Develop publicity posters or flyers for a school event

_____ Persuade others to sign a petition

_____ Plan advertising for a school or community newspaper

_____ Read business magazines

_____ Serve as a leader of a group

_____ Join the debate club or do public speaking

_____ Help run a school fair or carnival

_____ Ask for clothes, food, or other goods for people who need them

_____ Recruit members for a club

_____ Read newspapers

_____ Be the treasurer of a club or group

_____ Ask for donations to a community organization

_____ Campaign for a friend who is running for a school office

_____ Work as a salesperson or clerk at a charity store

_____ Sell advertising space for a school fundraiser

Check the School Subjects or Activities That You Do Well in or Enjoy:

_____ Language	_____ Computers
_____ Writing	_____ Psychology
_____ Speech	_____ Business
_____ Mathematics	
_____ Accounting	

Group 15

Check the Work Activities That Interest You:

_____ Developing ways to control air or water pollution

_____ Using advanced math and computer programs to perform research

_____ Predicting weather by studying wind, temperature, and humidity

_____ Providing technical help to groups that study the environment

_____ Drawing and figuring out maps, graphs, and diagrams

_____ Studying past civilizations by examining their weapons, tools, pottery, clothes, and customs

_____ Dissecting plants or animals to study their features

_____ Predicting or measuring earthquakes

_____ Designing and planning how to build a bridge

_____ Developing new machinery to perform certain kinds of work

_____ Developing and testing new medications

_____ Helping people decide how to best use computers to solve problems

_____ Gathering historical and statistical data to predict future trends

_____ Conducting tests of an elevator's speed, brakes, and safety devices

_____ Operating laboratory equipment to perform tests

Check the Sentences That Describe You:

_____ I like to try out my own ideas.

_____ I like to give directions and instructions to others.

_____ I like to plan my own work.

_____ I like to make decisions on my own.

_____ I like to use my abilities.

Check the Free-Time Activities You Do Now or Might Like to Do:

_____ Collect rocks or minerals

_____ Experiment with a chemistry set

_____ Use computer software to change photographs

_____ Install home sound equipment

_____ Belong to a computer club

_____ Read science or computer magazines

_____ Visit museums or historic sites

_____ Campaign for political candidates or issues

_____ Serve as the president of a club

_____ Do a science fair project

_____ Care for sick animals

_____ Conduct experiments with plants

_____ Study the habits of wildlife

_____ Engage in amateur astronomy

_____ Read about new discoveries in medicine

Check the School Subjects or Activities That You Do Well in or Enjoy:

_____ Physics

_____ Biology

_____ Environmental Science

_____ Computer Programming

_____ Chemistry

_____ Social Studies

_____ Geography

_____ Advanced Mathematics

Group 16

Check the Work Activities That Interest You:

_____ Signaling engineers to begin a train run, stop the train, or change speed

_____ Giving landing and take-off permission and other information to airplane pilots

_____ Inspecting, adjusting, and controlling radio equipment and airport lights

_____ Flying an airplane or helicopter to transport passengers

_____ Teaching students how to fly a plane

_____ Directing the route of airplanes and making necessary route changes because of weather conditions

_____ Interviewing, hiring, and training a ship's crew

_____ Piloting a ship

_____ Driving a tractor-trailer truck to transport and deliver products over a long distance

_____ Driving a bus to transport passengers over a specific route in a city

_____ Driving an ambulance in emergency situations

_____ Driving a delivery service car or truck to bring packages and goods to customers

_____ Inspecting a train engine at the start and end of a shift, refueling and lubricating the engine as needed

_____ Inspecting cars, trucks, and other vehicles to find damages

_____ Collecting tickets, fares, and passes from passengers

Check the Sentences That Describe You:

_____ I like to give directions and instructions to others.

_____ I like to plan my own work.

_____ I like to make decisions on my own.

_____ I like to do things for other people.

_____ I like to use my abilities.

Check the Free-Time Activities You Do Now or Might Like to Do:

_____ Lead a group

_____ Put together or repair bicycles

_____ Repair the family car

_____ Read airplane or boating magazines

_____ Set up and operate a model train

_____ Operate a motorboat or jet ski

_____ Serve as a crossing guard

_____ Build model airplanes, cars, or boats

_____ Race midget cars or go-karts

_____ Operate a CB or ham radio

_____ Plan family recreational activities

_____ Play flight simulators on the computer

_____ Drive a tractor on a family farm

_____ Fly remote-control airplane models

_____ Read car magazines

Check the School Subjects or Activities That You Do Well in or Enjoy:

_____ Algebra

_____ Science

_____ Driver's Education

_____ Mathematics

_____ Geography

_____ English

_____ Industrial or Technology Education

_____ Computers

Calculate Your Assessment Results

Directions

Go back to Group 1 in the assessment. Count the total number of check marks you made in that group. Write the total number for Group 1 in the box below. Repeat this step for all 16 groups.

[ ] Group 1: Agriculture and Natural Resources

[ ] Group 2: Architecture and Construction

[ ] Group 3: Arts and Communication

[ ] Group 4: Business and Administration

[ ] Group 5: Education and Training

[ ] Group 6: Finance and Insurance

[ ] Group 7: Government and Public Administration

[ ] Group 8: Health Science

[ ] Group 9: Hospitality, Tourism, and Recreation

[ ] Group 10: Human Services

[ ] Group 11: Information Technology

[ ] Group 12: Law and Public Safety

[ ] Group 13: Manufacturing

[ ] Group 14: Retail and Wholesale Sales and Service

[ ] Group 15: Science, Technology, Engineering, and Mathematics

[ ] Group 16: Transportation, Distribution, and Logistics

Circle the groups on the previous page that have the three highest totals. Notice that each group now has a name, too. Write the number and name of the groups with the three highest totals in the spaces below, starting with the group with the highest total.

My Three Highest Career Interest Groups

First Choice: Group #:_____   Name: _____

Second Choice: Group #:_____   Name: _____

Third Choice: Group #:_____   Name: _____

Use Your Assessment Results

There are more than 1,000 different jobs in the U.S. economy. Sifting through that many job titles to find what you like would be difficult and time consuming. Fortunately, these jobs have been organized into the 16 different Career Interest Groups used in the assessment. These groups help you explore jobs more easily and efficiently. Jobs in the same group are alike in many ways, and people who work in the same group of jobs share similar interests.

Your top three career interest group choices identify career areas where you are most likely to find work that you would enjoy. The next step is to learn more about the jobs and work activities in your top three choices. This section contains two tools to help you get started:

▼ The Career Interest Groups Record

▼ The Career Interest Group Descriptions

The Career Interest Groups Record pages provide a place for you to record information about your top three career interest groups. Because you will use this information frequently when making future plans, the record is a way to keep the information handy.

The Career Interest Group Descriptions tell you about the work interests, activities, and environments for each career group. Because each career interest group contains many different jobs, the group descriptions are further broken down into subgroups.

The subgroups will help you focus on certain kinds of work within a career interest group that you might like. The first subgroup in most areas is called "Managerial Work." That means if you worked in the Managerial subgroup, you would direct and supervise people who work in that career interest area, such as a police chief managing all the officers in a department.

Reading the descriptions and recording your choices in your Career Interest Groups Record will help you get a broader understanding of your top three choices. These activities will also show you that within each group, you still have many paths you might follow.

Directions

To fill in your Career Interest Groups Record, follow these steps:

1. Write the group number and name of your top three choices (from page 20) on the lines provided.

2. Turn to the Career Interest Group Descriptions starting on page 23. Find and read the description for your first choice.

3. When you've finished reading, answer the questions about that choice on the lines provided in your record.

4. Repeat steps 2 and 3 with your second and third choice.

Career Interest Groups Record

1. What is your first career interest group choice?

_____

In your own words, describe the work activities that people in this group enjoy.

_____

_____

What subgroups would you like to work in and what work activities from those subgroups interest you?

_____

_____

_____

What places would you like to work in?

_____

_____

2. What is your second career interest group choice?

_____

In your own words, describe the work activities that people in this group enjoy.

_____

_____

What subgroups would you like to work in and what work activities from those subgroups interest you?

_____

_____

_____

What places would you like to work in?

_____

_____

3. What is your third interest group choice?

_____

In your own words, describe the work activities that people in this group enjoy.

_____

_____

What subgroups would you like to work in and what work activities from those subgroups interest you?

_____

_____

_____

What places would you like to work in?

_____

_____

Career Interest Group Descriptions

Group 1: Agriculture and Natural Resources

What Work Do People in This Group Like?

People in this group like jobs working with plants, animals, forests, or mineral resources. They prefer to work outdoors, engaged in physical work such as farming, fishing, or forestry. Some study plants, animals, rocks, or minerals.

What Work Would I Like?

Read the descriptions of the subgroups in this group and circle the ones that interest you.

Managerial Work: People in this subgroup operate businesses such as farms, ranches, hatcheries, nurseries, and drilling and mining operations.

Resource Science and Technology: People in this subgroup do research to learn more about plants, animals, and natural resources. They study ways to improve the processes involved in agriculture, drilling, and mining. They also work to preserve the environment. Much of their work is done in laboratories.

Farming: People in this subgroup raise plants or animals on a farm or ranch. They work with their hands and use a variety of tools and machinery. Most of their work is outdoors.

Nursery, Groundskeeping, and Pest Control: Some people in this subgroup care for trees, shrubs, and lawns. Others apply chemicals to control pests. They use a variety of tools and equipment.

Forestry and Logging: People in this subgroup maintain forests and extract wood from them. They use tools and machines to plant trees; control erosion; and cut down, inspect, and transport trees to sawmills and pulp mills.

Hunting and Fishing: People in this subgroup hunt, catch, trap, or gather animals and marine life. They primarily work outdoors, many of them aboard commercial fishing boats.

Mining and Drilling: People in this subgroup use drilling and excavating equipment to access and mine oil and other natural resources. They often work underground or on offshore drilling platforms.

Where Would I Work?

People in this group work in places such as forests, fish hatcheries, farms and ranches, plant and landscaping businesses, laboratories, oil fields, mines and quarries, parks, and government offices.

Group 2: Architecture and Construction

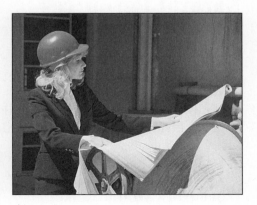

What Work Do People in This Group Like?

People in this group like jobs where they put up and finish buildings. Some are involved in planning and designing buildings. Others do work such as installing plumbing, using carpentry skills, laying bricks, painting, or roofing a building.

What Work Would I Like?

Read the descriptions of the subgroups in this group and circle the ones that interest you.

Managerial Work: People in this subgroup supervise and organize workers who build buildings, roads, or other structures. They are responsible for setting goals and making sure those goals are achieved.

Architectural Design: People in this subgroup plan and design buildings and landscapes. They make sure buildings are functional, affordable, and attractive.

Architecture/Construction Engineering Technology: People in this subgroup perform technical tasks, such as making detailed work plans, measuring and preparing maps of land and water areas, and inspecting buildings for problems.

Construction: People in this subgroup build structures. They put in the foundation and walls, floors, and roof. They also install parts such as the plumbing, electricity, windows, and insulation. They do work both inside and outside the building such as laying carpeting or putting in a driveway.

Systems and Equipment Installation and Repair: People in this subgroup repair and install electrical devices and systems that are a part of buildings and power and communication networks. They might work on appliances, motors, heating and cooling systems, or power lines.

Construction Support: People in this subgroup assist more skilled construction workers by performing a variety of tasks at construction sites. They might move materials, operate simple tools, and help maintain roadways and sewer systems.

Where Would I Work?

People in this group work in places such as construction sites, design studios, business offices, and streets and highways.

Group 3: Arts and Communication

What Work Do People in This Group Like?

People in this group like jobs where they can creatively express their feelings and ideas, communicate news or information, or work as performers.

What Work Would I Like?

Read the descriptions of the subgroups in this group and circle the ones that interest you.

Managerial Work: People in this subgroup plan, direct, and/or supervise the work activities of performers, artists, athletes, and other workers in all the subgroups of Arts and Communication.

Writing and Editing: People in this subgroup write stories, plays, articles, and poetry. They might also read and edit other people's work, making suggestions or changes to improve it. Others might write technical manuals.

News, Broadcasting, and Public Relations: People in this subgroup write factual information for newspaper and magazine articles and television news scripts. They also might report the news on television or radio. Sometimes their work includes convincing or persuading people to believe a certain point of view.

Studio Art: People in this subgroup draw, paint, or sculpt works of art.

Design: People in this subgroup design printed material such as advertisements, brochures, catalogues, or books. Others are involved in designing apparel, flowers, exhibits, and interior spaces. Still others design products such as cars and toys.

Drama: People in this subgroup perform for the public or direct performances and performers. Their work might include being in plays, movies, television shows, and other kinds of shows.

Music: People in this subgroup direct, compose, or perform instrumental or vocal music for the public. Others maintain and repair musical instruments.

Dance: People in this group use movement to express a story or an idea. Others choreograph dance routines or direct the performance of other dancers.

Media Technology: People in this subgroup operate the technical equipment needed to create photographs, movies, radio and television broadcasts, and sound recording.

Communications Technology: People in this subgroup use radio, telephones, and other technology to connect people and services.

Where Would I Work?

People in this group work in places such as newspapers and magazines; television, radio, movie, or recording studios; theaters and nightclubs; publishing companies, advertising agencies, and other business offices; and art and photography studios.

Group 4: Business and Administration

What Work Do People in This Group Like?

People in this group like making businesses or other organizations run smoothly. They work at all levels, from top executives to data entry. Some people in this group work a lot with business machines or computers while others work more with other people.

What Work Would I Like?

Read the descriptions of the subgroups in this group and circle the ones that interest you.

Managerial Work: People in this subgroup supervise and coordinate high-level business activities. They make business plans and see that they are carried out by doing tasks such as evaluating workers, planning budgets, ordering goods and services, and managing customer services.

Human Resources: People in this subgroup select, train, evaluate, and reward a business or organization's employees. They maintain personnel records and ensure that industry practices and government regulations are followed.

Secretarial Support: People in this subgroup do high-level clerical work requiring special skills and knowledge. They might advise customers or other workers, write reports, and work to improve management methods.

Accounting, Auditing, and Analytical Support: People in this subgroup manage money and the financial parts of a business. They collect and analyze financial information in order to help organizations make decisions.

Mathematical Clerical Support: People in this subgroup collect, organize, compute, and record numerical information used in business and finance.

Records and Materials Processing: People in this subgroup prepare, review, file, and organize recorded information. Others might check records and schedules for accuracy.

Clerical Machine Operation: People in this subgroup use business machines to record or sort information. They operate machines that type, print, sort, compute, send, or receive information.

Where Would I Work?

People in this group work in places such as business and government offices; stores and shopping malls; colleges and universities; travel agencies; courthouses; schools; doctors' and dentists' offices and clinics; factories and plants; hotels and motels; hospitals and nursing homes; auto service stations and repair shops; airports; country clubs and resorts; restaurants, cafeterias, and other eating places; and police and fire stations.

Group 5: Education and Training

What Work Do People in This Group Like?

People in this group like helping people learn. Many of them work as teachers at various levels. Others work in museums or libraries or provide counseling and health education.

What Work Would I Like?

Read the descriptions of the subgroups in this group and circle the ones that interest you.

Managerial Work: People in this subgroup are responsible for planning, budgeting, evaluating results, and supervising workers at colleges and school districts.

Preschool, Elementary, and Secondary Teaching: People in this subgroup do general and specialized teaching in classrooms, working with young children or teenagers.

Postsecondary and Adult Teaching: People in this subgroup teach specialized subjects to adults in a college, training, or workshop setting.

Library Services: People in this subgroup provide library services that connect people with information.

Archival and Museum Services: People in this subgroup acquire and preserve items of lasting value. They might catalogue, describe, or display these items.

Counseling, Health, and Fitness Education: People in this subgroup help other people lead healthy and well-directed lives, often by educating them to make educational and lifestyle changes. People in this subgroup also compete or officiate in team or individual athletic events.

Where Would I Work?

People in this group work in places such as schools and day care centers; schools or homes for people with disabilities; libraries, museums, zoos, and aquariums; and business and government offices.

Group 6: Finance and Insurance

What Work Do People in This Group Like?

People in this group like helping businesses and people secure their financial future. They use their knowledge of investments, economics, and risk to make sound financial decisions.

What Work Would I Like?

Read the descriptions of the subgroups in this group and circle the ones that interest you.

Managerial Work: People in this subgroup manage an organization's investments and cash. They also prepare financial forecasts and reports.

Investigation and Analysis: People in this subgroup evaluate financial information to help managers make decisions regarding financial transactions such as investments and insurance claims.

Records Processing: People in this subgroup verify, correct, file, and route important financial and insurance records.

Customer Service: People in this subgroup collect information; answer questions; and help customers fill out forms, make payments, and receive services.

Sales and Support: People in this subgroup sell services such as investment counseling, insurance, and advertising.

Where Would I Work?

People in this group work in places such as business and government offices, private homes, stores, and shopping malls.

Group 7: Government and Public Administration

What Work Do People in This Group Like?

People in this group like serving the needs of the public. They help keep the public safe by enforcing regulations, plan for public and community welfare, and provide the public with necessary services such as legal support and licensing.

What Work Would I Like?

Read the descriptions of the subgroups in this group and circle the ones that interest you.

Managerial Work: People in this subgroup are top-level and middle-level administrators who direct activities in government agencies and community organizations.

Public Planning: People in this subgroup plan the development of cities, towns, and rural areas. They also advise government officials on how to deal with economic, environmental, and social problems.

Regulations Enforcement: People in this subgroup protect the public by ensuring that products, facilities, and business practices are safe and legal.

Clerical Support: People in this subgroup perform various clerical duties that help courts, city governments, and licensing bureaus function.

Where Would I Work?

People in this group work in places such as government offices, courthouses, business offices, ports and harbors, factories and plants, office buildings, farms, railroad tracks and yards, hospitals and nursing homes, and streets and highways.

Group 8: Health Science

What Work Do People in This Group Like?

People in this group like jobs where they help people and animals to be healthy.

What Work Would I Like?

Read the descriptions of the subgroups in this group and circle the ones that interest you.

Managerial Work: People in this subgroup manage health-care activities. They might supervise health-care workers or provide leadership in running a hospital or nursing home. Many are involved with planning, budgeting, and staffing.

Medicine and Surgery: People in this subgroup diagnose and treat human diseases, disorders, and injuries.

Dentistry: People in this subgroup take care of patients' teeth and mouth tissue.

Health Specialties: People in this subgroup specialize in working with certain parts of the human body, such as eyes, feet, spinal column, or nervous system.

Animal Care: People in this subgroup care for and train many different kinds of animals.

Medical Technology: People in this subgroup use a variety of technical equipment to perform tests in order to detect signs of disease.

Medical Therapy: People in this subgroup plan and carry out treatment to improve the physical and emotional well-being of people. They also train people to continue their therapy at home.

Patient Care and Assistance: People in this subgroup are concerned about the physical needs of others. They help people do things they cannot do for themselves. They might care for people who are very young, who are very old, or who have handicaps.

Health Protection and Promotion: People in this subgroup help other people stay healthy and fit. They educate people to live healthier lifestyles, eat well, and exercise properly.

Where Would I Work?

People in this group work in places such as hospitals and nursing homes, schools and homes for people with disabilities, doctors' and dentists' offices and clinics, schools, drugstores, and health clubs.

Group 9: Hospitality, Tourism, and Recreation

What Work Do People in This Group Like?

People in this group like jobs where they fulfill the personal wishes and needs of other people. They might help people to enjoy good food and drink, to find a comfortable and clean place to stay away from home, or to participate in recreational activities.

What Work Would I Like?

Read the descriptions of the subgroups in this group and circle the ones that interest you.

Managerial Work: People in this subgroup manage all or part of the workers' activities in places such as restaurants, hotels, or other places where customers expect good service.

Recreational Services: People in this subgroup provide services to help other people enjoy a variety of recreational activities, from leading an exercise class to serving as a trail guide to dealing cards in a casino.

Hospitality and Travel Services: People in this subgroup help people who are traveling or vacationing plan trips and get acquainted with new surroundings.

Barber and Beauty Services: People in this subgroup cut and style hair or perform other services that improve personal appearance.

Food and Beverage Services: People in this subgroup prepare and serve food, greet customers, or keep restaurants clean and prepared for more customers.

Where Would I Work?

People in this group work in places such as hotels and motels; restaurants and cafeterias; hospitals and nursing homes; travel agencies; recreation centers and playgrounds; gymnasiums and health clubs; nightclubs, theaters, and amusement parks; airplanes, trains, and cruise ships; barber shops, beauty salons, and spas; country clubs and resorts; sports stadiums; and schools.

Group 10: Human Services

What Work Do People in This Group Like?

People in this group like improving people's social, mental, emotional, or spiritual well-being. They help people make personal decisions or solve personal problems. Many work exclusively with the young or the elderly.

What Work Would I Like?

Read the descriptions of the subgroups in this group and circle the ones that interest you.

Counseling and Social Work: People in this subgroup help people deal with their problems or life-changing events. Workers often specialize in problems that are personal, social, vocational, or physical in nature.

Religious Work: People in this subgroup conduct worship services, help people deal with spiritual problems, and provide religious education.

Child/Personal Care: People in this subgroup provide personal services to people who need a lot of attention, such as young children, people with chronic health problems, or people in mourning. They might provide companionship, household management, child care, and other forms of personal assistance.

Client Interviewing: People in this subgroup interview clients and business representatives to determine what services they need.

Where Would I Work?

People in this group work in places such as business and government offices, hospitals and nursing homes, houses of worship, colleges and universities, jails and reformatories, kindergartens and day care centers, private homes, and funeral homes.

Group 11: Information Technology

What Work Do People in This Group Like?

People in this group like designing, developing, managing, and supporting computer and information systems.

What Work Would I Like?

Read the descriptions of the subgroups in this group and circle the ones that interest you.

Managerial Work: People in this subgroup are responsible for managing complex computer resources and people who work with those resources. They use both technical and supervisory skills.

Information Technology Specialties: People in this subgroup use computer hardware and software to process information, solve problems, and conduct research.

Digital Equipment Repair: People in this subgroup repair and install digital electronic devices and systems such as computers, cash registers, ATMs, and copiers.

Where Would I Work?

People in this group work in places such as business and government offices, stores and shopping malls, factories and plants, hospitals and nursing homes, and anywhere else that computers are used extensively.

Group 12: Law and Public Safety

What Work Do People in This Group Like?

People in this group like jobs where they protect people, animals, and property. Some jobs give people authority, such as police or firefighters. They might do inspections or investigations or watch activities to make sure laws are followed. Others work in the legal system as lawyers, clerks, and judges.

What Work Would I Like?

Read the descriptions of the subgroups in this group and circle the ones that interest you.

Managerial Work: People in this subgroup manage fire and police departments. They set the goals and activities and make sure department members follow them. They also assign work duties and plan budgets.

Law: People in this subgroup apply their knowledge of the law to solve problems. They provide legal advice and representation, hear and decide on court cases, and help people and businesses reach legal agreements.

Legal Support: People in this subgroup investigate legal matters and prepare drafts of legal documents. They primarily provide support for lawyers and judges.

Law Enforcement and Public Safety: People in this subgroup enforce the laws and keep people safe. They might investigate suspicious people or behavior, prevent crimes, or find the causes of fires. They also inspect food, products, and buildings.

Safety and Security: People in this subgroup protect people, animals, and property. They keep watch to make sure that proper procedures are followed. They are also often responsible for preventing theft and vandalism.

Emergency Responding: People in this subgroup protect the public in case of emergency. They put out fires, treat and stabilize the sick or injured, and evacuate people from buildings.

Military: People in this subgroup serve in the armed forces of the United States. They might be in the Air Force, Army, Coast Guard, Marines, Navy, or National Guard. Their job is to keep peace and protect the United States in times of war.

Where Would I Work?

People in this group work in places such as federal, state, and local police and fire departments; government offices and courthouses; jails and reformatories; airports; private businesses such as factories, stores, hotels, and banks; and military bases in the United States and foreign countries.

Group 13: Manufacturing

What Work Do People in This Group Like?

People in this group like jobs where they make or repair products. They like to use their hands or hand tools or operate machines. They might inspect, count, or weigh products. Some of them might work for utilities that distribute power or other resources.

What Work Would I Like?

Read the descriptions of the subgroups in this group and circle the ones that interest you.

Managerial Work: People in this subgroup manage work in industrial and manufacturing plants. They supervise workers and set up the work tasks according to company policies and goals.

Machine Setup and Operation: People in this subgroup might set up industrial machines for others to operate or set up and operate the machines themselves. They monitor the machines' output and make necessary adjustments.

Production Work: People in this subgroup use various machines and equipment to modify materials such as leather, wood, stone, metal, plastic, and food. They might heat, cool, clean, coat, and shape them.

Welding, Brazing, and Soldering: People in this subgroup join metal parts together using torches, rivets, and other tools.

Production Machining Technology: People in this subgroup use machines to fashion metal or plastic parts. Others create molds, dies, and other machine parts to be used in production.

Production Precision Work: People in this subgroup create products with very precise requirements, such as jewelry, circuit boards, and eyeglass lenses.

Quality Control: People in this subgroup make sure that products conform to specifications and perform as they should. They pinpoint causes of defects and then help improve the manufacturing process.

Hands-On Work: People in this subgroup manufacture products using their hands and assorted hand tools.

Woodworking Technology: People in this subgroup cut, shape, and finish wood products such as furniture and cabinets. They follow very specific plans when they do this work.

Apparel, Shoes, Leather, and Fabrics: People in this subgroup clean, alter, restore, and repair clothing, shoes, and other apparel items.

Electrical and Electronic Repair: People in this subgroup repair and install electrical and electronic devices and systems, such as motors, appliances, power lines, and navigation systems.

Machinery Repair: People in this subgroup install, maintain, and repair various machinery and equipment, from industrial machinery to door locks and bicycles.

Vehicle Mechanical Work: People in this subgroup service and repair the bodies and engines of cars, trucks, buses, airplanes, boats, and ships.

Medical and Technical Equipment Repair: People in this subgroup repair sophisticated equipment requiring great precision, such as watches, cameras, and medical scanners.

Utility Operation and Energy Distribution: People in this subgroup operate systems that generate or distribute electricity, provide water or treat wastewater, or pump oil or gas.

Loading, Moving, Hoisting, and Conveying: People in this subgroup package or move products and materials using their hands, machinery, and other equipment.

Where Would I Work?

People in this group work in places such as factories and plants; waterworks, light, and power plants; airports; ports and harbors; oil fields; and freight terminals and warehouses.

Group 14: Retail and Wholesale Sales and Service

What Work Do People in This Group Like?

People in this group like jobs where they persuade customers to buy a product or use a service.

What Work Would I Like?

Read the descriptions of the subgroups in this group and circle the ones that interest you.

Managerial Work: People in this subgroup direct or manage sales activities or advertising programs for businesses and organizations.

Technical Sales: People in this subgroup sell products such as industrial machinery, computers and computer systems, and pharmaceuticals. They advise customers and help them pick what product or service is best for the customers' needs.

General Sales: People in this subgroup sell, demonstrate, or try to get orders for many different products or services. Some people spend all of their time in a single place, such as a department store. Others call on businesses or individuals.

Personal Soliciting: People in this subgroup appeal to people directly, either in person or on the phone, to buy a product or service. Usually they are interested in a one-time purchase only, not building a continuing relationship with the customer.

Purchasing: People in this subgroup buy goods and services, either for a business to use or to resell.

Customer Service: People in this subgroup work with customers in person. They might receive payments, collect information, answer questions, or help customers fill out forms.

Where Would I Work?

People in this group work in places such as business offices, stores and shopping malls, convention and trade show centers, factories and plants, doctors' and dentists' offices, laboratories, travel agencies, and private homes.

Group 15: Science, Technology, Engineering, and Mathematics

What Work Do People in This Group Like?

People in this group like jobs where they discover, collect, and study facts about the natural world. They use their knowledge of science, math, engineering, and technology to solve problems or improve how things are done.

What Work Would I Like?

Read the descriptions of the subgroups in this group and circle the ones that interest you.

Managerial Work: People in this subgroup plan, direct, and supervise the work activities of research scientists, engineers, and other workers in scientific, engineering, and math-related fields.

Physical Sciences: People in this subgroup generally work with things such as chemicals, rocks, and metals. They also study the movement of the earth and stars. Some workers test new theories. Others might develop new or improved materials for use in production and construction. These workers do a lot of research in fields such as geology, astronomy, oceanography, and meteorology.

Life Sciences: People in this subgroup do research and run experiments to learn more about plants, animals, and other living things. They use this knowledge to improve animal and plant species or to preserve the environment. Many of them are involved in medical research.

Social Sciences: People in this subgroup gather, study, and analyze information about human behavior. They might study individuals, small and large groups, and even whole societies. They study people and societies in the past and the present.

Laboratory Technology: People in this subgroup perform tests in laboratories in fields such as chemistry, biology, and physics. They record the information from their tests, so scientists, doctors, researchers, and engineers can use it.

Mathematics and Data Analysis: People in this subgroup do research and solve problems using advanced math, statistics, and computer programs. They analyze and interpret data for making decisions.

Engineering: People in this subgroup plan, design, and build bridges, buildings, roads, airports, air-conditioning systems, mining machinery, and many other things. They use scientific principles to develop ways to do their work. They usually specialize in one kind of engineering, such as civil, electrical and electronic, mechanical, mining, or safety.

Engineering Technology: People in this subgroup perform many technical activities to support engineering projects. They might make detailed drawings, measure and draw maps of land and water, or operate communications equipment. Other work might include inspecting buildings and equipment to make sure they are safe.

Where Would I Work?

People in this group work in places such as colleges and universities; factories and plants; waterworks, light, and power plants; mines and quarries; business and government offices and computer centers; farms and forests; zoos and aquariums; animal hospitals and laboratories; hospitals and nursing homes; and construction sites.

Group 16: Transportation, Distribution, and Logistics

What Work Do People in This Group Like?
People in this group like jobs where they move people or things over short or long distances.

What Work Would I Like?

Read the descriptions of the subgroups in this group and circle the ones that interest you.

Managerial Work: People in this subgroup manage transportation services, such as a whole airline, a bus system, or a subway system. They might supervise workers who drive trucks or work on cargo boats. They make sure people meet the goals and follow the policies set by the employer.

Air Vehicle Operation: People in this group fly airplanes or helicopters. They might also train and supervise other pilots.

Truck Driving: People in this subgroup drive large and small trucks and delivery vans. They might drive long distances between states, or they might follow a shorter, local route.

Rail Vehicle Operation: People in this subgroup drive trains, subway cars, and streetcars.

Water Vehicle Operation: People in this subgroup operate ships, boats, and barges. They pilot them, run the equipment, and see that passengers or cargo are handled well.

Other Services Requiring Driving: People in this subgroup drive smaller vehicles, mostly to take people from place to place. They might drive ambulances, taxis, or buses.

Support Work: People in this subgroup help with regular operations at airports, railroads, and docks. They might load and unload cargo or refuel and clean vehicles.

Where Would I Work?

People in this group work in places such as airplanes and airports, trains, bus and train stations, buses and trolleys, freight terminals, ports and harbors, railroad tracks and yards, ships and boats, and streets and highways.

Start an Individual Career Plan

You have now completed all the activities in Part 1 of *Pathfinder*. What have you learned? You know:

▼ More than 1,000 careers exist in the U.S. economy.

▼ Those careers can be divided into 16 career interest groups by the work people in each group like to do.

▼ The three career interest groups you like the most.

▼ The subgroups in your top three choices that most interest you.

▼ Work activities in those groups and subgroups that you like.

▼ Places that you might like to work.

That important knowledge is worth keeping. It will allow you to map future plans that match your interests. To make sure your personal information is not lost or forgotten, you will begin now to build a record of your choices. This record is called an *Individual Career Plan*, or *ICP*.

An ICP creates a permanent record of your interests and choices in one place. Each time you finish a part in *Pathfinder*, you'll add new information to your ICP. You can then use your ICP to make future plans. For example, you might use the information in your ICP to plan your high school courses, selecting classes to help you reach your career goals. You will probably use it to decide what kind of education or training you might like to pursue after high school. It can even help you select part-time jobs or volunteer activities.

To begin building your ICP, turn to page 112 now and fill in number 1 on your plan.

More Paths to Follow

Focusing Your Career Choices

In Part 1, you used the Career Interest Assessment to help you identify your top three career interest groups. You then selected subgroups within your top three choices that contained work activities you liked.

Part 2 will introduce you to other factors to consider when you match your interests with careers. These factors provide a clearer picture of which jobs within your top career interest areas might be satisfying for you:

▼ *What you enjoy spending most of your time working with*

▼ *Which work values are most important to you*

▼ *What kind of work environment you prefer*

▼ *What your physical abilities are*

▼ *If working in a nontraditional career or starting your own business is right for you*

When you finish this part, you will again record the choices you have made in your Individual Career Plan (ICP).

Data, People, and Things Choices

You now know that jobs can be grouped by the kinds of work activities people with those jobs do. Another method of grouping jobs is to put them in categories by *what* you will spend *most* of your time working with. The three main categories for this type of grouping are "Data," "People," and "Things." To understand what these categories mean, read the definitions for each category below.

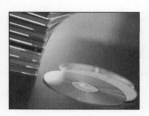

Data Careers

Some people like to work with data. Data includes things such as numbers, words, symbols, ideas, and concepts. Workers might put together lots of data to discover facts and develop new ideas or interpretations of ideas. They might gather, organize, and classify information to write reports or act on the data in some way. They examine and evaluate knowledge and information. Data work can involve computing, using math to figure out solutions, or planning actions. People who work with data like to do research and gather facts. They read, do tests or experiments, or interview people. They might also do research to make judgments. They might develop new ways to do things or create new products. People might also express their ideas artistically by designing, writing, or drawing. "Troubleshooting" is a type of data work. It means identifying and solving problems.

People Careers

Some people like careers working with others. ("People" work can also include working with animals if the animal is treated on an individual basis.) This work includes advising, counseling, or guiding other people to help them with problems. It can also mean exchanging ideas, information, and opinions with others to make decisions or draw conclusions. A lot of people work involves teaching others. It can include entertaining other people or persuading them to act in a certain way. Some workers supervise other people by leading their activities. People work also includes serving—acting on the needs or requests of other people.

Things Careers

Some people like to work with things. They spend a lot of time with machines, equipment, or tools. They might like to set up things. That means they prepare the equipment for work. Others might like to operate equipment. They start and stop it and control and adjust it while they work. Others might also tend machines or equipment while the machines are on. They might have to manipulate machines in certain ways to perform a job. Other things work includes driving or flying a variety of vehicles. Things work can also involve adjusting or repairing tools, machinery, and equipment.

Grouping Jobs by Data, People, and Things

Most jobs include work with data, people, and things. For example, read the following job description for social workers. You'll see how their work involves all three groups.

Social Workers: Social workers spend most of their time helping individuals, families, and groups try to solve their problems by talking with them (*people* work). They also read books, articles, and client reports to help solve problems. Often they use their reading to analyze their clients' problems (*data* work). Many social workers need to use a computer to write reports (*things* work).

Even though a social worker does data and things work, the job would be put in the "People" group. Why? Jobs are classified in these groups by what people spend most of their time working with, and social workers spend most of their time working with people. The activity below will help you further understand this type of grouping.

Directions

Read the job descriptions that follow. Decide whether you would put the job in the Data, People, or Things group. Make your decision by identifying what the workers spend most of their time working with: data, people, or things. (You can refer to the definitions on page 42 to help you decide.) On the line next to the description, write D for Data, P for People, or T for Things.

_____ 1. **Paralegals**
Paralegals gather information for lawyers. They help prepare cases for trial. They investigate the facts to find all important information. They also research and evaluate the facts to help lawyers decide whether a client has a good case. Paralegals talk with lawyers and court officers and interview clients.

_____ 2. **Automotive Body Repairers**
Automotive body repairers use machines and tools to fix damaged cars or small trucks. They straighten bent bodies and remove dents. Sometimes they replace damaged parts that can't be fixed. Body repair work is challenging. Each damaged car presents a different problem. Repairers use troubleshooting skills to figure out the right method to repair each car.

3. **Respiratory Therapists**

_____ Respiratory therapists diagnose lung and breathing problems by giving tests to patients. They check the test results to see whether the lungs are working right. They also gather facts to give lung treatments to people with breathing problems. Therapists also teach patients and their families how to use special breathing equipment at home. They might also make emergency visits to homes to troubleshoot problems.

4. **Firefighters**

_____ Firefighters respond to fire alarms to put out fires. They have to drive fire trucks and use complex firefighting equipment. Firefighters also try to prevent fires. They gather facts by inspecting buildings. They look for things that might cause a fire. They also educate people by speaking about fire prevention at schools and other places. Firefighters must write reports on the causes of fires. They study fire science books to keep up on the newest firefighting methods.

5. **Fashion Designers**

_____ Fashion designers express their ideas artistically. They design all kinds of clothing, such as coats, suits, dresses, and shoes. They gather information about what people like. Then they design and create clothes to match people's desires. Designers talk with lots of people in the fashion business to figure out fashion trends. They often present their designs to buyers or a design director. They try to persuade these people to select their designs.

6. **Plumbers**

_____ Plumbers use a variety of tools to put in and repair plumbing in homes and buildings. They also put in plumbing fixtures such as bathtubs, sinks, and toilets. Plumbers need troubleshooting skills to figure out and solve problems when the plumbing doesn't work right. They also must follow directions on building plans and blueprints to make sure their work is done correctly.

Now you know another way to identify jobs that might interest you. Would you like a job where you work primarily with data, people, or things? Think about which of these groups interest you the most. Record your choices in the box below.

My Data, People, and Things Choices

I would like a career where I work the most with _____

I would also not mind working with _____

I would least like to work a lot with _____

Work Values Choices

A *value* is something that's important to you. Different careers allow you to make choices about what you value the most. Although you might have many values in common with other people, how important a certain value is to you may differ from other people. For example, you might really like to do your work alone while others might prefer to work with other people. You probably would not mind spending some time working with other people, but what you value the most is being able to work by yourself. As you get older and begin to make choices about careers, your values might change. However, your values are something useful to think about now, too. If a job fits your values, you'll like it better. The list that follows can help you identify some value choices you will probably make when selecting a career.

Directions

Read each value description carefully. Check each value that you consider important. When you are done, look at the items you checked. Decide which three are your most important values. Circle your top three choices and label them #1, #2, and #3. Record your choices in the box at the end of this activity.

____1.   **Achievement:** I would like a job where I get a feeling of accomplishment.

____2.   **Activity:** I would like a job where I am busy all the time.

____3.   **Independence:** I would like a job where I can do my work alone.

____4.   **Variety:** I would like a job where I have something different to do every day.

____5.   **Compensation:** I would like a job where I get high pay when compared to most workers.

____6.   **Security:** I would like a job where I know I won't be laid off.

____7.   **Advancement:** I would like a job where I can get promotions.

____8.   **Recognition:** I would like a job where the work I do is appreciated.

____9.   **Authority:** I would like a job where I give directions to other workers.

____10. **Social Status:** I would like a job where I am looked up to by people I work with and people in the community.

____11. **Coworkers:** I would like a job where my coworkers are easy to get along with, and I'm not competing with them.

____12. **Social Service:** I would like a job where I do things for other people.

____13. **Moral Values:** I would like a job where I don't have to go against my sense of right and wrong.

____14. **Creativity:** I would like a job where I can try out my own ideas.

____15. **Responsibility:** I would like a job where I can make decisions on my own.

My Top Three Work Values

My first work value choice is _____

My second work value choice is _____

My third work value choice is _____

Work Environment Choices

A *work environment* means *where* you will work. Obviously different jobs have different locations, but they might have similar environments. Most people just assume they will work in some sort of building—an office or factory or hospital, for example. Yet many jobs are not performed in buildings. Even jobs that take place in similar environments can have different working conditions. Your work environment and working conditions can affect how you like your job. When choosing a career, you should consider what the work environment and work conditions will be.

The Basic Choices: Inside, Outside, or Both

Directions

The most basic decision about a work environment is whether you want to work inside, outside, or both. Read the descriptions and circle the one basic choice that you would most prefer. Then record your work environment choice in the box on the next page.

Inside: You will work inside a building or something that protects you from the weather. You might not be protected from temperature changes, however.

Outside: You will work outside with no protection from the weather.

Both: You will work about half the time inside and the other half outside.

Conditions to Consider

Job environments can have working conditions you may want to avoid. For example, you might not want a job that's dangerous, but other people wouldn't mind danger.

Directions

Read the following descriptions of other working conditions. Cross out any working condition that you would find unacceptable. Then record your work environment choices in the box on the next page.

Very Hot or Very Cold: Job conditions can include working in temperatures above 90 degrees or below 32 degrees Fahrenheit.

Noise Levels: Job conditions can include noise levels that are so high they can distract you from your work or make you uncomfortable.

Bad Lighting: Job conditions can include very bright light or poor lighting, making it difficult to see.

Hazards: Job conditions might include working in situations or with equipment that can cause injury or even death, or the job could harm your health.

Vibration: Job conditions could include using machinery that would cause your whole body to shake.

Fumes, Odor, Dust: Job conditions could make you uncomfortable or maybe cause injury.

Cramped Work Space: Job conditions might include working in spaces where you have to get into awkward positions.

Radiation: Job conditions might include the chance of being exposed to radiation.

Diseases/Infections: Job conditions could expose you to germs causing illness.

High Places: Job conditions might include working more than eight feet off the ground.

My Work Environment and Conditions Choices

Of the three basic choices, Inside, Outside, or Both, I would most like a job working

_____

I could put up with an environment that includes these conditions (record any conditions you did not cross out):

_____

_____

_____

_____

_____

I do not want to work in an environment that includes these conditions (record any conditions you crossed out):

_____

_____

_____

_____

_____

Physical Needs Choices

Some jobs might require lifting heavy boxes, climbing ladders, or walking a lot. Other jobs might require good eyesight or hearing. You might not like or be able to do a job because of its physical requirements. Considering the physical requirements of a job is another way to choose a job that is right for you. Some job lists include codes on the physical requirements needed to do the job. If physical requirements are important to you, have your teacher or counselor help you find job lists with physical requirement codes.

Directions

Read the following descriptions. They explain some physical requirements for jobs. At the end of the activity, record any choices you have. (If you do not have any physical needs requirements, skip this activity and go on to the next page.)

Vision: Jobs are coded by whether normal vision is needed; limited vision is needed; or no vision is needed. People who are blind can perform jobs where no vision is needed.

Hearing and Speech: Jobs are coded by whether normal hearing and speech are needed; limited hearing and speech are needed; or no hearing is needed. People who have no hearing or severely limited hearing could perform jobs where no hearing is required.

Lifting: Some jobs require people to lift heavy objects often. Jobs are coded to tell you about the lifting demands. Codes range from "Very Heavy," where you might lift over 100 pounds, to "Sedentary," where 10 pounds is the most you would have to lift.

Walking or Mobility: Jobs are coded by whether walking or mobility is required to do the work. People who use wheelchairs or have trouble walking could not perform these jobs. If a job does not have a walking or mobility code, people who use wheelchairs or have trouble walking could work at them.

My Physical Needs Choices

I would like a job that does not physically require me to

_____

Nontraditional Career Choices

A nontraditional career choice is working in a job that is usually done by the opposite gender. For example, a male nurse and a female carpenter are in nontraditional careers. When exploring careers you might like, make sure you are guided by your interests, not your gender.

Directions

Read the newspaper article that follows about Margie Seals's nontraditional career choice. Margie is a real person, and this article ran in newspapers across the country.* When you finish reading the article, answer the questions about Margie on the next page.

Woman brakes old tradition, achieves success as mechanic

ATLANTA (AP) - Margie Seals graduated from automotive school at the top of her class. She was the only woman among 1,000 students, and she couldn't get a job. "One shop owner," she said, told her to " 'fill out this application and drop it in the wastebasket when you get to the door.' He was one of the more honest ones."

When she finally got a job at a tune-up shop, the manager said, " 'The only reason I'm hiring you is because I couldn't hire a man with your credentials for what I'm about to pay you,' " Margie recalled.

Then things changed. Ms. Seals became the boss.

"When I started out, even women didn't want women working on their cars," she said, during a break between customers. "Today, it's part of my success."

Women account for 70 percent of the regular customers who bring their cars to My Favorite Mechanic, Inc., which opened in January.

"The feedback I keep getting is they can trust me," Ms. Seals said of her customers. "Plus, we're very good at what we do. You know the old saying: a woman has to be twice as good as a man."

Ms. Seals said she had trouble finding women to hire.

It took her a year before turning up Mary Jones, 41. She distributed 5,000 posters advertising "Women Mechanics Wanted" before Dianne Patterson, 29, came on board. Ms. Seals also employs two men and says business is booming.

At a time when more and more women are breaking into job fields once dominated by men, experienced women auto mechanics remain rare. Only 7,000 of 864,000 mechanics in the country are women, according to the U.S. Bureau of Labor Statistics.

Before she opened her shop, Ms. Seals, 38, ran a garage on wheels, making house calls; most of her customers were professional women.

When Margie Seals finished mechanic's school, she couldn't find a job; now she owns a garage.

She had plenty of business but had to turn down the big jobs that couldn't be done on the spot. After six years, she decided to set up shop.

Raven Wolfdancer, who has been entrusting his vehicles to Ms. Seals for four years, said, "I would prefer that no one else touch my car. I think it's a plus that she's a woman."

As she dropped off her Honda, Harriet Treadwell, a customer of three years, said, "Some men really do take advantage of women. Margie explains everything to you, not like you're an idiot."

Ms. Seals couldn't get a bank loan, so she cleaned out her savings, sinking $7,945 into her business.

She rattles off her credentials: four years in the U.S. Army, where she was in charge of keeping vehicles combat-ready, and six years as a motor transport service analyst for the Georgia transportation department. She is two courses away from an associate's degree in automotive technology and offers free lessons in car care.

* This article reprinted with permission from the Associated Press.

1. What problems did Margie have when she was looking for a job? Were they caused by her gender?

   _____

   _____

   _____

   _____

2. Why did someone finally hire her?

   _____

   _____

   _____

3. What factors led to Margie's success?

   _____

   _____

   _____

4. Margie's success encouraged her to become an *entrepreneur* (on-tre-pre-nur). An entrepreneur is someone who operates his or her own business. Margie started two businesses. Describe them.

   _____

   _____

   _____

5. How did Margie get her training to become a mechanic?

   _____

   _____

   _____

6. How is Margie continuing to improve her skills as a mechanic?

   _____

   _____

   _____

My Nontraditional Careers and Entrepreneurship Choices

Note: Responses here are optional. If you don't have any of these interests, just go on to the next section.

On the lines that follow, list any nontraditional careers that interest you or that you might like to learn more about.

_____

_____

_____

Also write down your thoughts about being an entrepreneur. Would you like to own your own business? What would you like to do? Why?

_____

_____

_____

_____

Individual Career Plan Additions

You now have other information that can help you choose career paths that are right for you. Part 2 of *Pathfinder* explored other choices to consider when selecting a career you'll like. You now know about

▼ Working with data, people, or things

▼ Considering work values that match your personal values

▼ Identifying different work environments and conditions

▼ Finding jobs that fit your physical requirements

▼ Choosing nontraditional careers or entrepreneurship

That's more important knowledge to record in your Individual Career Plan. To continue building your ICP, turn to page 112 now. Fill in numbers 2 through 7 on your plan.

After finishing the first two parts of *Pathfinder*, you now have the tools to explore career paths that match your interests. All the information you've gathered is recorded in your ICP. After exploring educational paths in Parts 3 and 4, you'll use this newfound knowledge to research specific careers you might like.

PART 3

Educational Paths Now

*Linking Core Academic
Skills and Careers*

This part of Pathfinder *will help you explore a vital path in your life—the educational choices you make. The educational choices you make now can determine what career paths will be open to you in the future. Your schoolwork now—the classes you take, how hard you work, the grades you get, and how you get along with other people—is connected to the careers you will work at as an adult. This part of* Pathfinder *will show you how these things are connected.*

At this time in your life, the law requires you to attend school. Have you ever thought about why our country has such laws? It's because our society recognizes how very important it is to have educated citizens. Your required schooling is designed to teach you core academic skills—the ability to read, write, compute, and think analytically and logically. Those core skills build a foundation that prepares you to perform the work in any job you choose as an adult. They also give you the skills necessary to be a contributing member of a democratic society. To understand the link between core academic skills and work, turn the page and begin the activities in Part 3.

Taking Tests to Get the Job

When you apply for a job—even as a high school student—you might have to take a test to get the job. Many employers use "pre-employment tests" ("pre-" means before you are hired). If you don't do well on the test, you probably won't get the job.

Pre-employment tests check your core academic skills. These skills show your ability to read, to use math, and to reason (think logically). They are called "core" for two reasons:

▼ Practically all jobs require reasoning, math, and language skills on at least a basic level.

▼ The core academic skills are the base you need to learn any new skills required for a particular job.

That's why all students must take classes in subjects such as English, math, and science.

On the next three pages, you'll find samples of two real pre-employment tests. To get a job at these stores, you would need to do well on the tests. Take them now and see how they check your core academic skills.

Pre-employment Test #1

Directions

This test is used by a large chain of grocery stores. It is given to all people applying for any job at its store—baggers, cashiers, bakery workers, managers, and others. High school students or adults who want part-time or full-time work must take the test. The whole test is 4 pages long and contains 68 questions. The store manager was asked why the store uses the test. He said, "This test helps us find the best people to hire, and that's what we want." Take the test now.

1. Subtract the following:

   a. $1.67   b. $5.32   c. $39.70   d. $83.11
      − .78   − 1.38   − 13.92   − 29.37

2. A customer wishes to buy a case of pears selling at 4 cans for $4.17. The case contains 12 cans. How much should you charge the customer? _____

3. Fill in the exact price per pound for each of the prices given below. Be sure to include fraction amounts in your answers.

   Example: 3 lbs. for $.25   Price per pound = $.083

                                                      Price per pound

   a. 3 lbs. for $1.09   _____

   b. $\frac{1}{4}$ lb. for $.36   _____

   c. 4 lbs. for $1.79   _____

   d. $\frac{1}{2}$ lb. for $1.63   _____

   e. 6 lbs. for $4.25   _____

4. A customer has $10.00. She wants to buy 8 apples at $.50 each. She would like to purchase grapes at $1.20 per pound. With the remaining money, how many pounds of grapes can she purchase? _____

5. Given the taxable subtotals below, calculate the appropriate tax for each. Then add the tax to the subtotal to find the total bill. The appropriate tax rate is 6 percent.

   a. $9.72   b. $2.13   c. $12.71   d. $38.71

   Tax: _____   Tax: _____   Tax: _____   Tax: _____

   Total: _____   Total: _____   Total: _____   Total: _____

6. A man brings a package of 3 green peppers to you. One pepper weighs 5 oz., one pepper weighs 6 oz., and one pepper weighs 9 oz. The total package retails at $3.20. The man would like the 2 largest peppers. How much will you charge him?

   _____

Pre-employment Test #2

Directions

This test is used by a bookstore. It is given to all high school students or adults who want full-time or part-time work at the store. Take the test now.

1. In what subject area would the following be found?

   a. A book on weight loss _____

   b. A book on remodeling _____

   c. A book on etiquette _____

2. Under what subject would books by the following authors be classified?

   Ansel Adams _____

   Carl Jung _____

   Bill Watterson_____

   John Bartlett_____

   Benjamin Spock_____

   Beverly Cleary_____

   Clive Cussler_____

   Arthur Miller _____

   Stephen Hawking_____

   C.S. Lewis _____

   Alice Walker _____

   Jean-Paul Sartre_____

   Frank Lloyd Wright _____

   Larry McMurtry _____

   Mary Oliver_____

   David McCullough _____

   Stephen R. Covey _____

   Jodi Picoult _____

   Arthur Frommer _____

   Claude Monet _____

   Tom Clancy _____

   Thomas Hardy_____

   Stephen King _____

   Wayne W. Dyer _____

   Chaucer_____

   P.D. James _____

   James Herriot _____

   Mo Willems _____

   Emily Dickinson _____

   Arthur Agatston _____

3. Put the following names in alphabetical order.

R. Kowalski   B. Crocker   W. Schemmel   G. Smith

W. Buckley   J. Thompson   D. Smith   L. McMurtry

J. Wambaugh   J. Mason   Fodor   J. Ellis

1. _____   7. _____

2. _____   8. _____

3. _____   9. _____

4. _____   10. _____

5. _____   11. _____

6. _____   12. _____

4. What is the selling price of a book if the retail price is $15.00 and we give a 20 percent discount? _____

5. What would be the selling price of a half-price paperback if the retail price is $7.95?

_____

What Do Pre-employment Tests Show You?

Directions

Answer the questions that follow about the two pre-employment tests you just took. They'll show you why academic skills are important.

1. Did you know that you might have to take tests on academic subjects before getting a job? What surprised you the most about these tests?

   _____

   _____

   _____

2. What academic subjects helped you answer the questions on both tests?

   _____

   _____

   _____

3. On the bottom of Test #1, the test evaluator marks the beginning, ending, and elapsed time of the test taker. "Elapsed time" means how long it took to take the test. What skill is the evaluator checking by recording the elapsed time? Why is this important?

   _____

   _____

   _____

4. On Test #2, you had to alphabetize a list of names. Did you alphabetize by the first or last name? If you used the first name, you did it wrong. Why do you need to use the last name?

   _____

   _____

   _____

5. The bookstore manager said that many people alphabetize incorrectly. Some use the first name, but most use the last name, yet they still don't get the names in the right order. The manager won't hire a person who doesn't alphabetize correctly. Even though people who take the test know the alphabet, why do you think they get this wrong?

_____

_____

_____

_____

6. What skill is the manager looking for on the alphabetizing question besides putting items in alphabetical order?

_____

_____

_____

_____

7. Why do you think both tests have math questions on them?

_____

_____

_____

_____

8. What have you learned from these tests about the connection between schoolwork and jobs?

_____

_____

_____

_____

Linking Core Academic Skills and Jobs

The pre-employment tests proved that employers want employees with good academic skills. So your math, English, science, and social studies classes are directly linked to future career choices. If you ever asked yourself, "Why do I need this class?" you now have the answer.

The world of work is always changing. That means you, as a worker, will be facing change constantly. To meet that challenge, you need the core academic skills; they give you the ability to learn and develop new skills. They are your foundation. Without them, you will not be able to keep up with the changing workplace.

The U.S. government believes these skills are so important that it organized a large group of people to decide which skills young people need to succeed in the world of work. They wrote a long report called the "SCANS" report. The report stated that to be successful, young people must have a solid foundation in the basic, core academic skills. The report defined these skills and grouped them into two major categories: basic skills and thinking skills.

Basic Skills

Students must be able to read, write, use arithmetic and mathematics, listen, and speak.

- ▼ **Reading:** This skill is the ability to locate, understand, and figure out written information in articles and books and in documents such as manuals, graphs, and schedules.

- ▼ **Writing:** This skill is the ability to clearly communicate thoughts, ideas, information, and messages in well-organized writing and create documents such as letters, directions, manuals, reports, graphs, and flow charts.

- ▼ **Arithmetic/Mathematics:** This skill is the ability to perform basic computations and approach practical problems by choosing the right mathematical technique.

- ▼ **Listening:** This skill is the ability to receive, pay attention to, understand, and respond to spoken messages and other cues.

- ▼ **Speaking:** This skill is the ability to organize ideas and communicate them out loud.

Thinking Skills

Students must be able to think creatively, make decisions, solve problems, visualize, know how to learn, and reason.

▼ **Creative Thinking:** This skill is the ability to come up with new ideas.

▼ **Decision Making:** This skill is the ability to choose the best method to get something done.

▼ **Problem Solving:** This skill is the ability to recognize problems and come up with ways to solve them.

▼ **Seeing Things in the Mind's Eye:** This skill is the ability to imagine or visualize something.

▼ **Knowing How to Learn:** This skill is the ability to use effective methods of gaining new knowledge and skills and then to apply that knowledge.

▼ **Reasoning:** This skill is the ability to make judgments, draw conclusions, or make evaluations and use them when solving a problem.

Making the Connection: Core Academic Skills and Schoolwork

You just read definitions explaining the core academic skills important for work. You learn those skills during your required schooling from kindergarten through high school. Let's put those definitions to work and see how your classes help you achieve those skills.

Directions

Each core academic skill listed on the next two pages has lines under it with the heading "Class/Assignment." On the lines, name a class and explain an assignment that required you to use that academic skill. Here is an example:

Writing: This skill is the ability to clearly communicate thoughts, ideas, information, and messages in well-organized writing and create documents such as letters, directions, manuals, reports, graphs, and flow charts.

Class/Assignment: Science class. I wrote a report on black holes.

1. **Reading:** This skill is the ability to locate, understand, and figure out written information in articles and books and in documents such as manuals, graphs, and schedules.

   Class/Assignment:

   _____

   _____

2. **Writing:** This skill is the ability to clearly communicate thoughts, ideas, information, and messages in well-organized writing and create documents such as letters, directions, manuals, reports, graphs, and flow charts.

   Class/Assignment:

   _____

   _____

3. **Arithmetic/Mathematics:** This skill is the ability to perform basic computations and approach practical problems by choosing the right mathematical technique.

   Class/Assignment:

   _____

   _____

4. **Listening:** This skill is the ability to receive, pay attention to, understand, and respond to spoken messages and other cues.

   Class/Assignment:

   _____

   _____

5. **Speaking:** This skill is the ability to organize ideas and communicate them out loud.

   Class/Assignment:

   _____

   _____

6. **Creative Thinking:** This skill is the ability to come up with new ideas.

   Class/Assignment:

   _____

   _____

7. **Decision Making:** This skill is the ability to choose the best method to get something done.

   Class/Assignment:

   _____

   _____

8. **Problem Solving:** This skill is the ability to recognize problems and come up with ways to solve them.

   Class/Assignment:

   _____

   _____

9. **Seeing Things in the Mind's Eye:** This skill is the ability to imagine or visualize something.

   Class/Assignment:

   _____

   _____

10. **Knowing How to Learn:** This skill is the ability to use good learning methods to learn and apply new knowledge and skills.

    Class/Assignment:

    _____

    _____

11. **Reasoning:** This skill is the ability to make judgments, draw conclusions, or make evaluations and use them when solving a problem.

    Class/Assignment:

    _____

    _____

Evaluating Your Core Academic Skills

Of course, all schools measure whether you are learning the core academic skills you will need for the future. The most frequent measurements you get are your grades on the assignments you do and the grades you receive for the classes you take at the end of each grading period. You also may take proficiency tests that tell you whether you are gaining the skills you need at a particular grade level. If you are not performing at least at a "C" level in your core academic classes, you are probably not learning skills you will need for the future.

Directions

On the lines below, write the names of the classes you are currently taking. Then, next to the class, estimate the grade you would receive in that class if your teacher gave you a final grade right now. Finally, decide whether you could do better by circling either "Yes" or "No."

1. Class_____ Grade_____

   I could do better in this class: Yes   No

2. Class_____ Grade_____

   I could do better in this class: Yes   No

3. Class_____ Grade_____

   I could do better in this class: Yes   No

4. Class_____ Grade_____

   I could do better in this class: Yes   No

5. Class_____ Grade_____

   I could do better in this class: Yes   No

6. Class_____ Grade_____

   I could do better in this class: Yes   No

Do you have grades lower than a "C"? Did you say you could do better in certain classes—that your grade does not represent your best work? If either is true, your grades or efforts are probably connected to other core skills that will be examined next. Using those skills can help you improve your academic skills.

Work Habits and Interpersonal Skills

Doing your best in academic classes depends a lot on your work habits and interpersonal skills. In fact, it's almost impossible to separate good work habits, good interpersonal skills, and academic achievement. "Work habits" refer to how you do your work; "interpersonal skills" refer to how you get along with others. These skills are vitally important for success in school and success at whatever job you choose.

Employers demand good work habits, such as getting to work on time and meeting deadlines. They also look for good interpersonal skills, such as getting along with others and following instructions. These skills and work habits are so important that the "SCANS" report listed them as personal skills students need to develop to be good workers:

▼ **Responsibility:** This quality means you try hard and don't give up before you complete a task.

▼ **Self-Esteem:** This quality means you believe in your ability to accomplish a goal if you work at it.

▼ **Sociability:** This quality means you understand other people, are friendly, and can adjust to others' ways of looking at things.

▼ **Self-Management:** This quality means that you know your own abilities, set personal goals, check your progress, and show self-control.

▼ **Integrity/Honesty:** This quality means you know the difference between right and wrong and act on those beliefs.

Personal Skills and Employee Evaluations

Work habits and interpersonal skills are so important that each year, most employers evaluate their workers on these personal skills. These evaluations are similar to getting a report card. They are often used to decide whether an employee will get a promotion or raise or be fired. The next activity shows a sample evaluation.

Directions

Read the employee evaluation of Jesse Craig on the next page. As you read, underline any words that describe Jesse's work habits or how he works with other people. Then list these work habits and interpersonal skills on the provided lines.

Richards and Wright, Inc.
Annual Evaluation: *Work Habits and Interpersonal Skills*

Employee: Jesse Craig
Position: Records Clerk
Years Employed: 3
Date: June 2011
Evaluator: Sandra Rothstein, Manager

Jesse is a dependable worker. I can count on him to get his work done well and on time. He is productive, getting a lot of work finished each day. His records are usually in order and neatly organized. On his own, he developed an efficient system to keep track of records that are out of the files and being used by other employees. Jesse takes on new tasks with a positive attitude. He is always willing to pitch in and help others when they get overloaded with work or when they get rush orders. He is responsible. I can count on him to get his work done without constant supervision. Personally, he is friendly, considerate of others, gets along well with other people in the office, and rarely engages in office gossip. Jesse is punctual, always arriving at work on time, and has few absences.

Rating: 10 = Highest, 1 = Lowest

(10) 9 8 7 6 5 4 3 2 1

_____

_____

_____

_____

_____

_____

_____

_____

Evaluating Your Work Habits and Interpersonal Skills

The work habits and interpersonal skills Jesse used in his job (that led to his high rating) are the same skills you need to be a successful student. The classroom is now your workplace. Developing good habits now will make you a good student and a valuable employee.

Directions

Evaluate your "in school" work habits and interpersonal skills. Read each of the following statements. Rank your skill level on a scale of 1 to 10 (10 = highest, 1 = lowest). Circle the number to show your ranking.

1. **I am a dependable worker.** I get my homework done and turn it in on time. I try to do a good job with my assignments. If teachers ask me to do something, I'll get it done.

    10 9 8 7 6 5 4 3 2 1

2. **I am punctual.** I get to school on time and am hardly ever tardy. I am not absent very often.

    10 9 8 7 6 5 4 3 2 1

3. **I get along well with others.** I don't make fun of other people. I do not judge people by their race, ethnic group, or religion. I don't spread gossip. I don't get in arguments or fights. I try to be friendly to everyone. I show respect to my teachers.

    10 9 8 7 6 5 4 3 2 1

4. **I am a productive worker.** I use my study time wisely. I get my work done without wasting time.

    10 9 8 7 6 5 4 3 2 1

5. **I am responsible.** I always have the supplies I need, such as pencils and paper, to do my work. I remember to write down my assignments and take home the books I need. I take good care of my schoolbooks and don't lose them.

    10 9 8 7 6 5 4 3 2 1

6. **I work well without supervision.** If the teacher is out of the room or busy with another student, I still do my work. I don't take advantage of the teacher and goof around when I should be working.

    10 9 8 7 6 5 4 3 2 1

7. **I have a positive attitude toward my schoolwork.** I don't always complain and say that I hate school, or that class is boring, or that my teacher hates me. I try to do my best even if the work is hard for me. If I'm having trouble with a subject, I ask for help.

10 9 8 7 6 5 4 3 2 1

8. **I show initiative.** I do my work and accept tasks without having to be told again and again to get to work. I try to plan ahead and make sure I have enough time to study for tests and finish assignments. I offer helpful suggestions.

10 9 8 7 6 5 4 3 2 1

To score your test, add all the numbers you circled to get your total points. Write your total on the line below. Use your total to find your overall work habits and interpersonal skills rating.

Your Total Score: _____

Work habits and interpersonal skills ratings:

> 80–73 = Excellent
>
> 72–65 = Good
>
> 64–49 = Average
>
> 48 and below = Poor

Your Rating: _____

Connecting Academic Achievement to Work Habits and Interpersonal Skills

If your rating on the evaluation was excellent or good, you are on your way to high academic achievement and to becoming a valuable employee! If your score is average or poor, you need to further develop some skills. You also need to realize how an average or poor rating on certain work habits probably prevents you from doing your best work or directly causes low grades. To understand that connection, follow these steps:

1. List three academic classes from page 64 where your grade is below a "C" or where you are not doing your best work.

   _____

   _____

   _____

2. List the three work habits or interpersonal skills where you rated yourself the lowest on pages 67–68. (Remember the scale was 10 = highest, 1= lowest.)

   _____

   _____

   _____

3. Decide whether your poor work habits or interpersonal skills identified in Step 2 cause your poor academic achievement in any way. Look at the descriptions on the evaluation for help. Explain how these work habits affect your achievement on the lines below.

   For example: I don't do my math homework very often. When I get to class, I don't know what the teacher is talking about. So I don't pay attention.

   _____

   _____

   _____

   _____

   _____

   _____

   _____

4. Carefully review what you wrote in Step 3. On the lines in the box below, set three goals for yourself that will help you improve your work habits and academic achievement.

For example: I will write down all my assignments and make sure I bring home the books I need to do them.

Goals for Improvement

1. _____

_____

2. _____

_____

3. _____

_____

More Information for Your Individual Career Plan

Part 3 of *Pathfinder* showed you that your schoolwork now is directly linked to your future career choices. You've learned that

▼ Your classes in core academic skills—such as math, English, science, and social studies—develop your reasoning, math, and language skills. Those skills are needed for all jobs.

▼ Good personal qualities, such as work habits and interpersonal skills, are needed in school and at work.

▼ Academic achievement is directly linked to good work habits and interpersonal skills.

▼ Improving work habits will improve academic achievement.

This knowledge is important for your Individual Career Plan. It will help do your best work developing your core academic skills. To add this data to your plan, turn to page 115 now. Fill in number 8.

Postsecondary Educational Paths

Choosing the Right Path for You

Part 4 focuses on your postsecondary educational choices. "Postsecondary" means the education you choose after high school. Unlike the required schooling covered in Part 3, postsecondary choices are not required by law. They are strictly up to you. You decide whether you want to continue your education, what kind of schooling you want, where you will go to school, and how many years you will devote to postsecondary education. Also, you have to pay for postsecondary education; it's not free like your required education.

When you graduate from high school, you will have a lot of important choices to make. Part 4 is designed to help you make the choices that are right for you. The following activities will help you explore the many available postsecondary educational options. Because different jobs have different postsecondary education requirements, you'll need to connect your career interests from Parts 1 and 2 with your educational choices. Knowing what level of education is required for jobs that interest you allows you to make informed choices.

Let's see what the future holds for you. Turn the page and start your first activity.

Job-Related Skills for the Future

Any career will require learning skills beyond your core academic and personal skills. For example, a computer programmer must know how to write programs for computers. A court reporter has to know how to use a special typing machine, called a stenotype, to quickly type what is said in court. A nurse has to know how to administer shots. A police officer must learn how to use a firearm. These skills are called "job-related" because you need them to work at a specific job. Sometimes, these skills are learned on the job. Many other jobs may require special training or education to learn the job-related skills.

You may have heard people say, "You can't get a good job anymore unless you go to college." That is not true. First of all, what is a "good" job? The answer to that question depends on the person. A "good" job will be defined by your interests, needs, and values. (That's why you spent a lot of time in Parts 1 and 2 exploring these things.) Your definition of a good job will probably be different from other people's definitions.

What is true, however, is that many jobs in our economy are now more complex and have ever-changing demands. Thus, they require training or education beyond high school. There are many ways besides going to college to get that training or education. To explore the possibilities open to you, first read about the three basic paths you can choose. The next several pages explore possible choices within each path.

The Technical/Trade Path

If you choose this path, your education will focus solely on learning job-related skills for a specific career or career area. While in high school, you will be taking classes to improve your core academic skills. However, some high schools do offer classes where you can begin learning job-related skills. Different high schools offer many technical/trade preparation choices for their students.

Your teacher or counselor will explain the choices available at your school. Technical/trade preparation is often continued after high school. Such education or training focuses on learning more advanced job-related skills. This choice generally does not require taking further classes in the core academic skills. Further education and training following the technical/trade path can be as short as a few weeks or as long as several years, depending on the choices you make within this path. The many choices for technical/trade preparation after high school are explained later.

The Associate Degree Path

This path is like a bridge between the technical/trade path and the college preparatory path. When pursuing an associate degree, you usually take classes both to further develop core academic skills and learn job-related skills. You may choose this path because you want to develop advanced skills for a specific job that requires an associate degree. You may also choose this path as the first step in attending a college or university. You need to discuss this choice with your parent(s), teachers, and counselors. The course of study you choose for an associate degree will help you plan what courses to take in high school.

The College Preparatory Path (or "College Prep")

If you know your goal is to immediately go to a college or university after high school, choose this path. During high school, your education will focus on developing advanced core academic skills. Colleges do not accept all students who apply. To be accepted, you need to take certain courses in high school. You will also need to maintain a good grade point average and take college entrance exams such as the ACT or SAT. A college prep program makes sure you take the right courses to get accepted and to be prepared for college work. A college or university degree focuses on developing high-level skills in both the core academic areas and job-related areas. College or university degrees usually take four years to complete if you attend school full-time. A college education is expensive these days, so be sure to discuss this choice with your parent(s) and counselors. Many students need financial aid to attend college, so you want to be sure you are ready to make this investment in your future.

The next several pages provide more in-depth discussion of these three paths. This information can help you choose the path that best matches your desires and career interests. Remember, however, that your goals may change as you grow older. That's why it's useful to learn about all the paths open to you.

Exploring the Technical/Trade Path

The technical/trade path includes going to work right after high school or continuing your education after high school to obtain more job-related skills. If you want to get a job right after graduating, choose your career area as soon as possible. Then take as many job-related courses as you can during high school. If you decide to continue your technical or trade training after high school, many programs last less than two years. If you want more training, many other choices exist. Here are some of the options:

Co-op Programs: Some high schools allow you to work while still in high school to get on-the-job experience. For example, a student taking business courses might work in an office.

On-the-Job Training: In this training, job-related skills are learned by doing the work. Also, you often have an experienced worker showing you what to do. Some employers now use videos to help train their workers. On-the-job training can be short, moderate, or long term. Short-term training can be little as a few days or weeks to learn the necessary job skills. Moderate-length training can be from 1 to 12 months. New workers often observe experienced workers perform tasks. Then the new workers are gradually moved into harder tasks. Long-term training generally requires an apprenticeship, which is described next.

Apprenticeship: An apprenticeship provides both work experience and education and training for people entering a specific occupation. In an apprenticeship program, you learn job-related skills through classroom instruction and on-the-job training. Training can last between one and four years. Apprenticeships are offered by sponsors who hire and train the apprentice.

Employer-Sponsored Training: Some jobs require very specific job-related training that can only be obtained from the employer. A police officer, for example, must attend a police academy and pass the coursework before getting that job. Flight attendants must also take specific training required by the airline for which they work.

Vocational, Business, and Technical Schools: Many schools provide job-related training after high school. These schools offer training programs for many different jobs. Most of the programs last from three months to two years. Your studies will focus on skills needed for a specific job. Such schools frequently offer courses to provide hands-on experience. You will take few, if any, core academic classes. These schools also help students get a license or specific credential if it is needed for a certain job.

Military Training: All military service branches offer specific job-related training for a variety of jobs. If you do well in the training, you may work in a military job using those skills. Many military jobs are the same as jobs in the nonmilitary workforce. That means the skills you learn at your military job can be used in civilian jobs when you leave the military. Thus you get both training and job experience.

Does the Technical/Trade Path Interest You?

Directions

Write your answers to the questions on the lines provided below. Your answers will help you decide whether you want to follow this path.

1. Does the technical/trade path sound interesting to you? (Yes or No) _____

   (If you answered "Yes," complete the questions that follow. If you answered "No," go on to the next page.)

2. Would you like to continue your education after high school? (Yes or No)_____

3. What kind of training interests you from the list on page 74? (You can be interested in more than one type.) Why does this interest you?

   _____

   _____

   _____

   _____

4. What do you like the most about the technical/trade path?

   _____

   _____

   _____

   _____

5. What do you like the least about the technical/trade path?

   _____

   _____

   _____

   _____

Exploring the Associate Degree Path

An associate degree usually takes two years of education after high school. This degree prepares you for a specific job or entry into a career field such as business. However, you are also required to take advanced core academic skills classes. If you decide to go on to a college or university, these core classes will apply toward your college degree. This process is called "transferring credit." Schools that offer the two-year associate degree include the following:

Community and Junior Colleges: These two-year colleges often offer a wide variety of courses and programs. Many programs will lead to an associate degree, while other programs may lead to a training certificate. When you earn a degree here, you can later transfer many of your credits toward a four-year degree if you choose.

Business Colleges and Private Vocational Schools: Some privately owned schools offer two-year associate degree programs. The programs offered are like those at community colleges, although they generally require fewer core academic skills classes. However, the credits earned at these schools often will not apply toward a four-year degree. Before enrolling in any of these schools, make sure to check whether the credits will transfer.

Does the Associate Degree Path Interest You?

Directions

Write your answers to the questions on the lines provided below. Your answers will help you decide whether you want to follow this path.

1. Does the associate degree path sound interesting to you? (Yes or No) _____

   (If you answered "Yes," complete the questions that follow. If you answered "No," go on to the next page.)

2. Why does the associate degree path appeal to you?

   _____

   _____

   _____

3. What do you not like about the associate degree path?

_____

_____

Exploring the College Prep Path

The college prep path ("prep" is a shortened form of the word "preparatory") means you will take high school classes that prepare you for studies at a four-year college. The kind of work you will do for a four-year degree is explained below.

Colleges and Universities: You can earn a four-year college degree at many colleges or universities. Universities are like four-year colleges but are often larger and offer more programs. Both offer a wide variety of courses to take.

Colleges and universities require you to take advanced core academic courses during the first year or two. You will also select a *major*—a field of study that interests you the most. Once you choose a major—such as English, business, computer science, or art—you take advanced courses in this area, too. Your major may prepare you for a specific job, such as a teacher. Majors may also prepare you for jobs in a career area such as business.

When you have finished your studies, you will receive a bachelor's degree. This process usually takes about four years if you attend school full-time. Then you will look for a job in an area related to your major.

Online Colleges and Universities: Online colleges and universities offer classes over the Internet instead of at a particular location. An online college usually offers the same materials and classes as other colleges. (Many colleges and universities now offer both in-person and online courses.) Internet schooling is becoming more acceptable to employers, and students like it because of the flexibility it offers. However, if you're interested in an online school, ask your counselor for help to make sure the school is *accredited.* That means the school's programs have been approved by an outside agency. (You also should make sure that this agency is recognized by the U.S. Department of Education.) Accreditation also makes credits more likely to transfer to other schools.

College Prep+

A college prep+ path means you are interested in an occupation where you will need to pursue further education after receiving a bachelor's degree. If you want to be an architect, a veterinarian, or a dentist, for example, you must have additional schooling. Advanced degrees are obtained in two places:

Graduate Schools: Graduate schools are often part of a larger university. They offer advanced degrees in many subjects. A master's degree usually takes two years of education beyond the bachelor's degree. The doctorate degree often takes several years of specialized education beyond the master's degree.

Professional Schools: A professional school provides the advanced education needed for certain careers. A lawyer, for example, has to go to law school after college. A doctor must attend medical school. Many of these careers also require you to get experience, pass special exams, or get a license before you can do the work.

Does the College Prep Path Interest You?

Directions

Write your answers to the questions on the lines provided below. They will help you decide whether you want to follow this path.

1. Does the college prep path sound interesting to you? (Yes or No) _____

   If you answered "No," why?

   _____

   _____

   If you answered "Yes," complete the questions that follow. If you answered "No," go on to the next page.

2. Do you have any idea what you might like to major in during college? If so, name the major and explain why it interests you. If you can't name a major, just explain an area that interests you.

   _____

   _____

3. Would you rather go to work after college, or go on to graduate or professional school? Why?

_____

_____

_____

4. What do you like the most about the college prep path?

_____

_____

_____

5. What do you like the least about the college prep path?

_____

_____

_____

Understanding Career Development: Be Ready for Change!

When you start high school, you'll choose a technical path or a college prep path. You might even change your mind during high school and switch paths. That's fine, because your interests will change as you get older. Even after you graduate from high school and get a job, you might want to choose another path. That's fine, too. As you gain job experience, your interests will grow and change. Think of your first job as the first step in your career development. You can decide to continue your education or training to make changes in your plans. Read Kim's story next. It's a good example of how career development works.

Directions

Read the story. As you read, underline all the career choices Kim makes: the degrees she earns, the job she gets, and her future plans. You will do an activity based on your underlining.

Kim had always enjoyed drawing. She really liked to sketch cars, airplanes, and buildings, and invent new designs for them. Through a career assessment, she learned that her career interests were in the mechanical and design areas. When planning her high school courses in the eighth grade, Kim wasn't sure whether she wanted to go to a four-year college. So she selected a technical/trade path. Her high school offered courses in an engineering/industrial cluster. This path let her learn skills in drafting and design. At the same time, she built her academic skills. When choosing her academic classes, her counselor helped her pick classes that would also prepare her for college.

By tenth grade, Kim had enjoyed her technical classes so much that she decided to continue on her technical/trade path and not go to college. She changed her high school plan to include more drawing and design classes. At first she wanted to be an architectural drafter after graduating from high school. An architectural drafter works with an architect to design, draw, and plan new building projects such as apartments or schools. Or architects and architectural drafters may work on fixing up older buildings.

But as she researched that career, Kim changed her mind. She learned that employers like to hire drafters with training beyond high school. Her chances of getting a job would be better with advanced training. She also learned that she would make more money and have a better chance for promotions with advanced training.

Another thing Kim discovered was most drafting jobs involved using special computer programs called "CAD" (Computer-Aided Design). Even though Kim had used computers to draw designs in high school, she felt she needed to learn more about CAD. So after graduating, Kim went to a community college. She got an associate of arts degree in architectural technology. This degree took two years to finish.

After earning her associate degree, Kim got a job with a construction company. Her first big project was working on an addition to a local hospital. Kim was glad she had training in computers. Much of the design for this project was done on computers.

Since earning her degree, Kim has taken more classes in CAD at a nearby university. Her job experience has shown her she will need this knowledge. It also has shown her that computer design programs are constantly changing, so to keep up, she has needed more classes. She has also discovered how much she likes designing on computers. At work, Kim has learned a lot about the work done by architects, architectural engineers, and civil engineers. She thinks that someday she might go back to school. She would like to earn a four-year bachelor's degree in computer science, engineering, or architecture.

How Did Kim's Career and Educational Plans Change?

Directions

Kim made many decisions about her school and career plans. List her decisions in chronological order. Start with her first career and educational interests and end with her future plans. Use your underlining in the story to build your list.

_____

_____

_____

_____

_____

_____

_____

_____

_____

_____

_____

_____

_____

_____

_____

_____

More Information for Your Individual Career Plan

Part 4 of *Pathfinder* helped you explore the many postsecondary school choices available to learn job-related skills. You've learned that

▼ Any career you choose will require you to learn job-related skills. Those are the skills needed to work at a specific job. You may choose from several education or training paths to learn job-related skills. Planning those choices starts in high school.

▼ Your three main postsecondary educational choices are the technical/trade path, the associate degree path, or the college prep path.

▼ Each of the three paths has further choices within it to get the education or training you want.

▼ You should plan your high school classes to match your postsecondary educational interests.

▼ Your career plans can grow and change throughout your life. Continued education or training will help you plan further career development.

This knowledge is important for your Individual Career Plan. Parts 3 and 4 have explored the role your schooling plays in selecting careers. Part 4 has focused on educational choices you will make after graduating from high school. Your new knowledge about your career interests and educational interests will help you choose careers that match your educational plans. To add this data to your plan, turn to page 115 now. Fill in number 9.

Career Research

Matching Career Interests and Educational Choices with Jobs

Parts 1 and 2 of Pathfinder *helped you make choices about your career interests. Part 3 showed you the importance of core academic skills for any job. Part 4 introduced the concept of job-related skills and described different paths where you can learn those skills. Part 5 will make the final connection by bringing both your career and educational choices together to help you match your choices with specific jobs. You will make this match through research.*

Through research, you'll be able to make informed decisions about the educational paths to follow to obtain your career goals. You'll learn about the work people do at a particular job and the education or training they needed to get that job. You'll also learn many other interesting facts about particular jobs, such as salary, work environment, and growth projections.

You may be assigned to research only one or two jobs—but you can do more on your own! The more you know about different careers and their required education or training, the better you will be able to plan your high school career and beyond.

How Do You Research Specific Jobs?

Doing "research" means that you use various sources, such as books or the Internet, to find information about a subject. Of course, the subject you're interested in here is job information. However, the research process is the same, no matter what your subject is. Research is an easy task once you know how to do it. Here are the steps:

1. Decide what you want to research. In this part, you will research specific job titles. To help you make your decision, this part contains a list of titles organized by the 16 career interest groups and their subgroups in Part 1. The title list begins on page 86.

2. Decide what research methods you will use. Descriptions of the many sources to get career information begin on page 104.

3. Record the information you find. Use the Career Research Record beginning on page 106 to write down information you find about the job. If you need more copies of this record, you teacher will give them to you.

You see, research is as easy as 1-2-3! Now, go to the next section to get started.

Select a Job Title to Research

To select a job title that reflects your career and educational interests, you will need to start by reviewing the interests you recorded in your Individual Career Plan.

1. What are your highest career interest groups (see number 1 on page 112)?

   First career interest group:

   _____

   Second career interest group:

   _____

   Third career interest group:

   _____

2. What subgroups in your three highest career interest groups interest you (see number 1 on page 112)?

   First career interest subgroups:

   _____

   _____

Second career interest subgroups:

_____

_____

Third career interest subgroups:

_____

_____

3. What is your educational path choice(s) (see number 9 on page 115)?

_____

4. In the following job lists, read the job titles in your three highest career interest groups and subgroups. Circle any job titles you would like to research. How many have you circled? _____

5. Because some of the titles will be unfamiliar to you, you may not choose them. You might miss a job you would really like, however, if you only select jobs that are familiar. To solve that problem, quickly check job descriptions of titles you don't know in your top career areas. The easiest way to do that is to use a search engine to look for the job title on the Internet. After reading short definitions of the unfamiliar job titles, circle the ones that sound interesting to you. How many circled job titles do you have now?

_____

6. Look at the jobs you circled. Do any of them have the same educational path you listed in step 3? _____ If so, underline the circled job titles that match the educational path you chose.

7. Review your circled job titles, and pick one title to research. If you are having trouble deciding, focus on the circled and underlined titles in your highest career interest group. Write the job title and education level here:

_____

_____

Of course, you can research more than one job. Your circled titles will help you pick more jobs to research later on. You may choose to research a job that matches your educational choices. Remember, though, that you may change your mind about your educational path. Thus, don't eliminate jobs on education alone. Researching jobs with educational paths different from your choices may help you more fully understand how your education and training choices affect the kind of work you will do. If you are unsure about the educational path you want to follow, looking at similar jobs with different educational paths may help you decide. Many job descriptions also will include core academic school subjects that are important for the occupation. That's useful knowledge for high school planning, too, and may further help you decide which educational path you will select.

Job Lists by Career Interest Groups, Subgroups, and Educational Paths

The following job lists are organized by the career interest groups and subgroups from Part 1 that you recorded on your ICP. The jobs listed here have a faster-than-average projected job growth. Some subgroups in a career interest group might not have any jobs with a predicted job growth. If that is true, the subgroup is not included in the job lists. The lists also give you the educational path recommended for that job. This educational path is the path that most people in this occupation have followed.

Directions

Use this list to pick a job to research from your three highest career interest groups. The following abbreviations are used to indicate the recommended educational path: T/T= Technical/Trade path; AD = Associate Degree path; CP = College Prep path; CP+ = College Prep plus a professional or graduate school path.

Group 1: Agriculture and Natural Resources

Job Title	Path
Managerial Work	
Agricultural Crop Workers Managers	CP
Animal Husbandry Workers Managers	CP
Farm Products Purchasing Agents	T/T
Farmers and Ranchers	T/T or AD or CP
Landscaping Managers	T/T
Nursery and Greenhouse Managers	CP
Resource Science and Technology	
Agricultural Engineers	CP
Agricultural Scientists	CP+
Animal Scientists	CP
Environmental Engineering Technicians	AD
Environmental Engineers	CP
Food Scientists and Technologists	CP
Mining and Geological Engineers	CP

Veterinarians	CP+
Zoologists and Wildlife Biologists	CP

Nursery, Groundskeeping, and Pest Control

Landscaping Workers	T/T
Nursery Workers	T/T
Pest Control Workers	T/T
Pesticide Applicators	T/T
Tree Trimmers and Pruners	T/T

Forestry and Logging

Park Naturalists	CP

Mining and Drilling

Excavating Machine Operators	T/T
Loading Machine Operators	T/T
Rock Splitters, Quarry	T/T

Group 2: Architecture and Construction

Job Title	Path

Managerial Work

Construction Managers	CP

Architectural Design

Architects	CP+
Landscape Architects	CP

Construction

Boatbuilders and Shipwrights	T/T
Boilermakers	T/T
Brickmasons and Blockmasons	T/T
Carpenters	T/T
Ceiling Tile Installers	T/T
Cement Masons and Concrete Finishers	T/T
Commercial Divers	T/T
Construction and Building Inspectors	T/T
Crane and Tower Operators	T/T
Electricians	T/T
Glaziers	T/T
Grader and Bulldozer Operators	T/T
Hazardous Materials Removal Workers	T/T
Manufactured Building Installers	T/T
Painters, Construction and Maintenance	T/T

Paving, Surfacing, and Tamping Equipment Operators	T/T
Pipelayers	T/T
Plasterers and Stucco Masons	T/T
Plumbers, Pipefitters, and Steamfitters	T/T
Reinforcing Iron and Rebar Workers	T/T
Roofers	T/T
Security and Fire Alarm Installers	T/T
Sheet Metal Workers	T/T
Stone Cutters and Carvers	T/T
Stonemasons	T/T
Terrazzo Workers and Finishers	T/T
Tile and Marble Setters	T/T

Systems and Equipment Installation and Repair

Electrical and Electronics Repairers, Powerhouse, Substation, and Relay	T/T
Elevator Installers and Repairers	T/T
Heating and Air-Conditioning Mechanics	T/T
Refrigeration Mechanics	T/T

Construction Support

Construction Laborers	T/T
Helpers—Carpenters	T/T
Helpers—Repair Workers	T/T
Highway Maintenance Workers	T/T

Group 3: Arts and Communication

Job Title	Path
Managerial Work	
Agents and Business Managers	CP
Art Directors	CP
Producers	CP
Program Directors	CP
Technical Directors	CP
Writing and Editing	
Copy Writers	CP
Creative Writers	CP
Editors	CP
Poets and Lyricists	CP
Technical Writers	CP

News, Broadcasting, and Public Relations
Caption Writers   T/T
Interpreters and Translators   CP
Public Relations Specialists   CP

Studio Art
Cartoonists   T/T or AD or CP
Craft Artists   T/T
Painters and Illustrators   T/T or AD or CP
Sculptors   T/T or AD or CP
Sketch Artists   T/T or AD or CP

Design
Commercial and Industrial Designers   CP
Desktop Publishers   T/T or AD or CP
Fashion Designers   AD
Floral Designers   TT
Graphic Designers   CP
Interior Designers   AD
Merchandise Displayers   T/T
Set and Exhibit Designers   CP

Drama
Actors   T/T or AD or CP
Costume Attendants   T/T
Directors   CP
Makeup Artists, Theatrical   T/T

Music
Composers   CP
Music Arrangers and Orchestrators   CP
Music Directors   CP
Musicians   T/T or AD or CP
Singers   T/T or AD or CP
Talent Directors   CP

Media Technology
Audio and Video Equipment Technicians   T/T
Broadcast Technicians   T/T or AD
Camera Operators   AD or CP
Film and Video Editors   CP
Multimedia Artists and Animators   CP
Professional Photographers   T/T or AD or CP
Sound Engineering Technicians   T/T

Communications Technology
Dispatchers   T/T

Group 4: Business and Administration

Job Title	Path
Managerial Work	
Administrative Services Managers	CP
Administrative Support Supervisors	T/T
Compensation and Benefits Managers	CP
Customer Service Supervisors	T/T
Financial Managers	CP
Human Resources Managers	CP
Meeting and Convention Planners	CP
Private Sector Executives	CP
Public Relations Managers	CP
Storage and Distribution Managers	CP
Training and Development Managers	CP
Human Resources	
Compensation, Benefits, and Job Analysis Specialists	CP
Employment and Placement Specialists	CP
Employment Interviewers	CP
Labor Relations Managers and Specialists	CP
Personnel Recruiters	CP
Training and Development Specialists	CP
Secretarial Support	
Executive Secretaries and Administrative Assistants	T/T or AD
Legal Secretaries	T/T
Medical Secretaries	T/T
Accounting, Auditing, and Analytical Support	
Accountants	CP
Auditors	CP
Budget Analysts	CP
Logisticians	CP
Management Analysts	CP
Market Research Analysts	CP
Survey Researchers	CP
Mathematical Clerical Support	
Billing, Cost, and Rate Clerks	T/T
Bookkeeping Clerks	T/T
Brokerage Clerks	T/T

Records and Materials Processing

Correspondence Clerks	T/T
Human Resources Assistants	T/T
Office Clerks, General	T/T
Production Clerks	T/T

Clerical Machine Operation

Billing and Posting Clerks and Machine Operators	T/T
Mail Clerks and Mail Machine Operators	T/T

Group 5: Education and Training

Job Title	Path

Managerial Work

Education Administrators, Elementary and Secondary School	CP
Education Administrators, Postsecondary	CP+
Education Administrators, Preschool	CP
Instructional Coordinators	CP+

Preschool, Elementary, and Secondary Teaching

Elementary School Teachers	CP
Kindergarten Teachers	CP
Middle School Teachers	CP
Preschool Teachers	AD
Secondary School Teachers	CP
Special Education Teachers, Middle and Secondary School	CP
Special Education Teachers, Preschool, Kindergarten, and Elementary School	CP
Teacher Assistants	T/T
Vocational Education Teachers	CP

Postsecondary and Adult Teaching

Adult Literacy, Remedial Education, and GED Teachers and Instructors	CP
Postsecondary Teachers	CP+
Self-Enrichment Education Teachers	T/T
Vocational Education Teachers, Postsecondary	T/T

Library Services

Librarians	CP+
Library Assistants, Clerical	T/T
Library Technicians	T/T

Archival and Museum Services

Archivists	CP+
Audiovisual Collections Specialists	CP
Curators	CP+
Museum Technicians and Conservators	CP

Counseling, Health, and Fitness Education

Athletes and Sports Competitors	T/T
Coaches and Scouts	T/T
Educational and Vocational Counselors	CP+
Fitness Trainers and Aerobics Instructors	T/T
Umpires, Referees, and Sports Officials	T/T

Group 6: Finance and Insurance

Job Title	Path

Managerial Work

| Financial Managers | CP |
| Treasurers, Controllers, and Chief Financial Officers | CP |

Investigation and Analysis

Appraisers, Real Estate	AD
Assessors	AD
Claims Examiners	T/T
Cost Estimators	CP
Credit Analysts	CP
Financial Analysts	CP
Insurance Adjusters and Investigators	T/T
Insurance Appraisers, Auto Damage	T/T
Insurance Underwriters	CP
Loan Counselors	CP
Loan Officers	T/T
Market Research Analysts	CP

Records Processing

| Insurance Claims Clerks | T/T |

Customer Service

Bill and Account Collectors	T/T
Loan Interviewers and Clerks	T/T
New Accounts Clerks	T/T
Tellers	T/T

Sales and Support

Job Title	Path
Advertising Sales Agents	T/T
Insurance Sales Agents	T/T
Personal Financial Advisors	CP
Sales Agents, Financial Services	CP
Sales Agents, Securities and Commodities	CP

Group 7: Government and Public Administration

Job Title	Path

Managerial Work

Administrative Services Managers	CP
Legislators	CP
Social and Community Service Managers	CP
Storage and Distribution Managers	T/T

Public Planning

City and Regional Planning Aides	AD
Urban and Regional Planners	CP+

Regulations Enforcement

Aviation Inspectors	T/T
Child Support, Missing Persons, and Unemployment Fraud Investigators	CP
Construction and Building Inspectors	T/T
Environmental Compliance Inspectors	T/T
Financial Examiners	CP
Fire Inspectors	T/T
Forest Fire Inspectors	T/T
Immigration and Customs Inspectors	T/T
Licensing Examiners and Inspectors	T/T
Occupational Safety Specialists	CP

Clerical Support

Court Clerks	T/T
License Clerks	T/T
Municipal Clerks	T/T

Group 8: Health Science

Job Title	Path
Managerial Work	
Coroners	T/T
Medical and Health Services Managers	CP
Medicine and Surgery	
Anesthesiologists	CP+
Family and General Practitioners	CP+
Internists	CP+
Medical Assistants	T/T
Medical Transcriptionists	T/T or AD
Obstetricians and Gynecologists	CP+
Pediatricians	CP+
Pharmacists	CP+
Pharmacy Technicians	T/T
Physician Assistants	CP
Psychiatrists	CP+
Registered Nurses	AD or CP
Surgeons	CP+
Surgical Technologists	T/T
Dentistry	
Dental Assistants	T/T
Dental Hygienists	AD
Dentists	CP+
Health Specialties	
Chiropractors	CP+
Optometrists	CP+
Podiatrists	CP+
Animal Care	
Animal Breeders	T/T
Animal Trainers	CP
Nonfarm Animal Caretakers	T/T
Veterinarians	CP+
Veterinary Assistants and Laboratory Animal Caretakers	T/T
Veterinary Technicians and Technologists	AD
Medical Technology	
Cardiovascular Technologists	AD
Diagnostic Medical Sonographers	AD or CP
Medical and Clinical Laboratory Technologists and Technicians	AD or CP

Medical Appliance Technicians	T/T
Medical Equipment Preparers	T/T
Medical Records Technicians	AD
Nuclear Medicine Technologists	AD
Opticians, Dispensing	T/T
Orthotists and Prosthetists	CP
Radiologic Technologists and Technicians	AD

Medical Therapy

Audiologists	CP+
Massage Therapists	T/T
Occupational Therapist Assistants	T/T or AD
Occupational Therapists	CP
Physical Therapist Assistants and Aides	T/T or AD
Physical Therapists	CP
Radiation Therapists	AD
Recreational Therapists	CP
Respiratory Therapists	AD
Speech-Language Pathologists	CP+

Patient Care and Assistance

Home Health Aides	T/T
Licensed Practical and Licensed Vocational Nurses	T/T or AD
Nursing Aides, Orderlies, and Attendants	T/T
Psychiatric Aides and Technicians	T/T

Health Protection and Promotion

Athletic Trainers	CP
Dietetic Technicians	T/T
Dieticians and Nutritionists	CP
Emergency Medical Technicians and Paramedics	T/T
Health Educators	CP
Occupational Health Specialists	CP
Occupational Health Technicians	AD

Group 9: Hospitality, Tourism, and Recreation

Job Title	Path

Managerial Work

Food Service Managers and Supervisors	T/T
Gaming Managers and Supervisors	T/T
Housekeeping Supervisors	T/T

Janitorial Supervisors	T/T
Lodging Managers	T/T
Supervisors of Personal Service Workers	T/T

Recreational Services

Amusement and Recreation Attendants	T/T
Gaming and Sports Book Writers and Runners	T/T
Gaming Dealers	T/T
Gaming Slot Key Persons	T/T
Locker Room and Coatroom Attendants	T/T
Recreation Workers	T/T
Ushers and Ticket Takers	T/T

Hospitality and Travel Services

Baggage Porters and Bellhops	T/T
Concierges	T/T
Flight Attendants	T/T
Hotel, Motel, and Resort Desk Clerks	T/T
Janitors and Cleaners	T/T
Maids and Housekeeping Cleaners	T/T
Reservation Ticket Agents	T/T
Tour Guides and Escorts	T/T
Transportation Attendants	T/T

Barber and Beauty Services

Hairdressers and Cosmetologists	T/T
Manicurists and Pedicurists	T/T
Shampooers	T/T
Skin Care Specialists	T/T

Food and Beverage Services

Bakers, Bread and Pastry	T/T
Bartenders	T/T
Chefs and Head Cooks	T/T
Cooks, Fast Food	T/T
Cooks, Institution and Cafeteria	T/T
Cooks, Restaurant	T/T
Cooks, Short Order	T/T
Counter Attendants	T/T
Food Preparation Workers	T/T
Hosts and Hostesses	T/T
Waiters and Waitresses	T/T

Group 10: Human Services

Job Title	Path
Counseling and Social Work	
Child, Family, and School Social Workers	CP
Clinical, Counseling, and School Psychologists	CP+
Health Educators	CP+
Medical and Public Health Social Workers	CP
Mental Health and Substance Abuse Social Workers	CP
Mental Health Counselors	CP
Probation Officers	CP
Residential Advisors	CP
Social and Human Service Assistants	T/T
Substance Abuse and Behavioral Disorder Counselors	CP
Social Science Research Assistants	AD
Religious Work	
Clergy	CP+
Directors, Religious Activities	CP
Child/Personal Care	
Child Care Workers	T/T
Embalmers	T/T
Funeral Attendants	T/T
Nannies	T/T
Personal and Home Care Aides	T/T
Client Interviewing	
Eligibility Interviewers, Government Programs	T/T
Interviewers, Except Eligibility and Loan	T/T

Group 11: Information Technology

Job Title	Path
Managerial Work	
Computer Systems Managers	CP
Network Administrators	CP
Information Technology Specialties	
Computer Programmers	CP
Computer Security Specialists	CP
Computer Software Engineers	CP
Computer Support Specialists	AD
Computer Systems Analysts	CP
Database Administrators	CP
Network Systems Analysts	CP

Group 12: Law and Public Safety

Job Title	Path
Managerial Work	
Forest Firefighting Supervisors	T/T
Municipal Firefighting Supervisors	T/T
Supervisors of Police and Detectives	T/T
Law	
Arbitrators, Mediators, and Conciliators	CP
Lawyers	CP+
Legal Support	
Court Reporters	T/T
Law Clerks	CP
Paralegals and Legal Assistants	AD
Law Enforcement and Public Safety	
Bailiffs	T/T
Correctional Officers and Jailers	T/T
Criminal Investigators	T/T
Fire Investigators	T/T
Forensic Science Technicians	CP
Highway Patrol Pilots	T/T
Police Detectives	T/T
Police Patrol Officers	T/T
Police Records Officers	T/T
Sheriffs and Deputy Sheriffs	T/T
Transit and Railroad Police	T/T

Safety and Security
Job Title	Path
Animal Control Workers	T/T
Gaming Surveillance Officers	T/T
Private Detectives and Inspectors	T/T
Security Guards	T/T
Transportation Security Screeners	T/T

Emergency Responding
Job Title	Path
Emergency Medical Technicians	T/T
Firefighters	T/T
Forest Firefighters	T/T

Military

If you are interested in a career in the armed forces—the Air Force, Army, Coast Guard, Marines, Navy, and National Guard—the best career information can be obtained from a recruiter in the particular branch that interests you.

Group 13: Manufacturing

Job Title	Path

Managerial Work
Job Title	Path
Supervisors/Managers of Helpers, Laborers, and Material Movers	T/T
Supervisors/Managers of Mechanics, Installers, and Repairers	T/T
Supervisors of Production Workers	T/T

Production Work
Job Title	Path
Bakers, Manufacturing	T/T
Meat, Poultry, and Fish Cutters	T/T
Packaging and Filling Machine Operators	T/T
Production Laborers	T/T
Slaughterers and Meat Packers	T/T

Welding, Brazing, and Soldering
Job Title	Path
Brazers	T/T
Solderers	T/T
Welders and Cutters	T/T

Production Machining Technology
Job Title	Path
Lay-Out Workers, Metal and Plastic	T/T
Model Makers, Metal and Plastic	T/T
Numerical Control Machine Tool Operators and Tenders, Metal and Plastic	T/T
Numerical Tool Programmers	T/T

Quality Control

Occupational Safety Specialists — CP

Hands-On Work

Painters, Transportation Equipment — T/T
Painting and Decorating Workers — T/T

Apparel, Shoes, Leather, and Fabrics

Laundry and Dry-Cleaning Machine
  Operators and Tenders — T/T
Precision Dyers — T/T

Electrical and Electronic Repair

Avionics Technicians — T/T
Electrical and Electronics Installers and
  Repairers, Transportation Equipment — T/T
Electrical and Electronics Repairers,
  Commercial and Industrial Equipment — T/T
Electronic Equipment Installers and
  Repairers, Motor Vehicles — T/T

Machinery Repair

Bicycle Repairers — T/T
Industrial Machinery Mechanics — T/T
Locksmiths and Safe Repairers — T/T

Vehicle Mechanical Work

Aircraft Body Repairers — T/T
Aircraft Engine Specialists — T/T
Aircraft Rigging Assemblers, Precision — T/T
Aircraft Structure Assemblers, Precision — T/T
Aircraft Systems Assemblers, Precision — T/T
Airframe and Power Plant Mechanics — T/T
Automotive Body and Related Repairers — T/T
Automotive Glass Installers and Repairers — T/T
Automotive Master Mechanics — T/T or AD
Automotive Service Technicians and
  Mechanics — T/T or AD
Bus and Truck Mechanics and Diesel
  Engine Specialists — T/T or AD
Mobile Heavy Equipment Mechanics — T/T
Motorboat Mechanics — T/T
Motorcycle Mechanics — T/T
Recreational Vehicle Service Technicians — T/T

Medical and Technical Equipment Repair

Medical Equipment Repairers — T/T

Utility Operation and Energy Distribution

Nuclear Power Reactor Operators — T/T or AD
Water Treatment Plant Operators — T/T

© JIST Publishing

Group 14: Retail and Wholesale Sales and Service

Job Title	Path
Managerial Work	
Funeral Directors	AD
Market Research Analysts	CP
Marketing Managers	CP
Property Managers	CP
Sales Managers	CP
Supervisors of Nonretail Sales Workers	T/T
Supervisors of Retail Sales Workers	T/T
Technical Sales	
Agricultural Sales Representatives	T/T
Chemical and Pharmaceutical Sales Representatives	T/T
Electrical and Electronic Sales Representatives	T/T
Instruments Sales Representatives	T/T
Mechanical Equipment and Supplies Sales Representatives	T/T
Medical Sales Representatives	T/T
Sales Engineers	CP
General Sales	
Real Estate Brokers	T/T
Real Estate Sales Agents	T/T
Retail Salespersons	T/T
Sales Representatives, Wholesale and Manufacturing	T/T
Personal Soliciting	
Demonstrators and Product Promoters	T/T
Models	T/T
Purchasing	
Purchasing Agents	T/T
Customer Service	
Adjustment Clerks	T/T
Cashiers	T/T
Counter and Rental Clerks	T/T
Customer Service Representatives	T/T
Gaming Cage Workers	T/T
Receptionists and Information Clerks	T/T

Group 15: Science, Technology, Engineering, and Math

Job Title	Path
Managerial Work	
Engineering Managers	CP
Natural Sciences Managers	CP
Physical Sciences	
Atmospheric and Space Scientists	CP
Chemists	CP
Environmental Scientists	CP+
Geologists	CP+
Geophysicists	CP+
Hydrologists	CP+
Materials Scientists	CP
Life Sciences	
Agricultural Scientists	CP+
Biochemists	CP+
Biologists	CP+
Biophysicists	CP+
Environmental Scientists and Specialists	CP
Epidemiologists	CP+
Medical Scientists	CP+
Microbiologists	CP+
Social Sciences	
Anthropologists	CP+
Archeologists	CP+
Economists	CP
Industrial-Organizational Psychologists	CP+
Social Science Research Assistants	AD
Sociologists	CP+
Laboratory Technology	
Biological Technicians	AD
Environmental Science Technicians	AD
Geological and Petroleum Technicians	AD
Photographers, Scientific	T/T
Mathematics and Data Analysis	
Actuaries	CP
Computer and Information Scientists, Research	CP+
Market Research Analysts	CP
Mathematical Technicians	CP

Mathematicians	CP+
Operation Research Analysts	CP+
Statisticians	CP

Engineering

Aerospace Engineers	CP
Biomedical Engineers	CP
Chemical Engineers	CP
Civil Engineers	CP
Electrical/Electronics Engineers	CP
Fire Prevention and Protection Engineers	CP
Health and Safety Engineers	CP
Industrial Engineers	CP
Marine Engineers	CP
Marine Engineers and Naval Architects	CP

Engineering Technology

Aerospace Engineering Technicians	AD
Calibration Technicians	AD
Cartographers and Photogrammetrists	CP
Civil Engineering Technicians	AD
Industrial Engineering Technicians	AD
Surveying and Mapping Technicians	T/T

Group 16: Transportation, Distribution, and Logistics

Job Title	Path

Managerial Work

Aircraft Cargo Handing Supervisors	T/T
Railroad Conductors and Yardmasters	T/T
Storage and Distribution Managers	T/T
Transportation Managers	T/T

Air Vehicle Operation

Air Traffic Controllers	T/T
Airfield Operations Specialists	T/T
Airplane Pilots and Flight Engineers	CP
Commercial Pilots	CP
Traffic Technicians	AD

Truck Driving

Tractor-Trailer Drivers	T/T
Truck Drivers, Heavy	T/T
Truck Drivers, Light or Delivery Services	T/T

Water Vehicle Operation

Captains or Mates of Water Vessels	T/T
Dredge Operators	T/T
Motorboat Operators	T/T
Sailors and Marine Oilers	T/T
Ship Engineers	T/T

Rail Vehicle Operation

Subway and Streetcar Operators	T/T

Other Services Requiring Driving

Ambulance Drivers and Attendants	T/T
Bus Drivers, School	T/T
Bus Drivers, Transit and Intercity	T/T
Taxi Drivers and Chauffeurs	T/T

Support Work

Cargo and Freight Agents	T/T
Cleaners of Vehicles and Equipment	T/T
Transportation Inspectors	T/T
Traffic Technicians	T/T

Where Can You Find Career Information?

You can find career information from many sources. These sources are explained here. As you do your research, write down the information you find on the Career Research Record that begins on page 106.

 **Directions**

Read about the different sources of career information. Then pick the ones you want to use. A teacher, counselor, or librarian can help you decide.

Occupational Outlook Handbook (OOH)

This excellent source of career information is a book that is published by the U.S. Department of Labor every two years. The *OOH* describes more than 300 jobs. Each job description has information on job duties, training and education needed, skills needed, working conditions, where to get additional information, and other details. Most school and public libraries have this book. It is also available free on the Internet at http://www.bls.gov/OCO/.

People You Know

People are a great source of information about careers. You can interview family members; relatives; and people in your neighborhood, school, and community about their jobs. Ask them what they like and do not like about their work. Find out how they got started in their field and what type of education or training they needed.

Job Shadowing

When you "job shadow," you go to work with a person who works at a job you might like. You watch all the work that person does. You may even do some of the work. Talking with the person and seeing what the person does help you to learn about that job. Your teacher or counselor may be able to help you arrange a job shadowing experience.

The Library

Your school and public libraries are another source of career information. Many books, reference materials, magazine articles, and software programs describe jobs. Your teacher, counselor, or librarian can help you find career information in books and other library sources.

Professional Organizations

Most careers have one or more professional organizations associated with them. One of the purposes of these organizations is for their members to share information about their careers with each other and other interested people. To find the names and contact information of the organizations related to the careers that interest you, look in the *Occupational Outlook Handbook*. Another good resource is *The Encyclopedia of Associations*, which you can find in most public libraries. Your teacher or librarian can help you find this information, too.

Most professional organizations have a website with a page for students that describes what people in that career do and what education or training is required. You can find these websites by typing the name of the organization into Google or another search engine. These organizations also will mail you career information if you write and ask for it.

Computer Software

Some schools and libraries have career exploration computer software. If your school or local library has this software, your teacher, counselor, or librarian can show you how to use it.

Career Resource Centers

Many schools and public libraries have special centers for all their career information. This includes books, videos, magazines, reference materials, and sometimes even career exploration software. If your school or local library has a career resource center, it is an excellent place to begin career research.

Job Fairs

Some schools and businesses hold job fairs. You can attend them to learn about careers. Job fairs usually have speakers who explain different careers. The speaker can answer specific questions about jobs. You can also get lots of free career materials. Ask your teacher or counselor about job fairs in your school or community.

The Internet

The Internet provides a huge number of job-related sites. Typing "career information" in an Internet search engine will result in hundreds of choices for information. Another option is to type a job title of interest into a search engine, such as Google, and explore the links that look most promising.

Career Research Record

Directions

Use this record to write down your research information. If you can't find the answers to some questions, you can skip them or try another source to find the answer. If you need another copy of this record, your teacher will give you one.

Career Information

Name: _____

School: _____

Grade: _____ Date: _____

Job title: _____

Career interest group and subgroup:_____

_____

1. What work activities would you do on this job?

   _____

   _____

   _____

2. Would you work mostly with data, people, or things on this job? Circle your answer.
   (Definitions are on page 42 if you need to refer to them.)

         Data   People   Things

3. Would this job match your data, people, or things choices? (See box on page 44.) Explain
   why or why not.

   _____

   _____

   _____

4. Describe the working environment and working conditions of this job.

   _____

   _____

   _____

   _____

5. Does this job match your work value choices? (See page 46.)Explain why or why not.

_____

_____

_____

6. Does this career fit your physical needs? (See box on page 49.) Explain why or why not.

_____

_____

_____

7. Is this a nontraditional job for your gender? (See page 50.) Circle your answer:

         Yes   No

8. Do you think you would be comfortable working at a nontraditional job? Explain why or why not.

_____

_____

_____

9. Could you be self-employed or run a small business with this job? Circle your answer:

         Yes   No

10. If you answered yes, would running your own business related to this career interest you? Explain why or why not.

_____

_____

_____

_____

11. What is the average pay for an entry-level person in this job?

_____

12. What is the job outlook for the future? ("Job outlook" predicts how many jobs of this type will be needed in the future. Your source may talk about job growth or give the outlook in percentages.)

_____

13. Does the outlook make a difference to you? Explain why or why not.

_____

_____

_____

14. What other jobs are related to this job?

_____

_____

15. If you got more education or training, what other jobs in this career area could you get?

_____

_____

Education or Training Information

16. What educational path is recommended for this job? Circle the most appropriate path (from the job list, which begins on page 86).

   Technical/trade   Associate degree   College prep   College prep+

17. What does your research source say is the training or education you will need for this job?

_____

_____

18. Look at the list of core academic skills on pages 60 and 61. Write down the skills listed there that you think you will need for this job:

_____

_____

19. What academic subjects should you take to make sure you have these skills? Does your source recommend taking any specific high school classes? List them on the lines provided:

_____

_____

_____

20. Can you take any technical classes in high school that will help you prepare for this job? List these classes on the lines below:

_____

_____

_____

21. List any test, license, or certification needed for this job.

_____

_____

Remember Your Individual Career Plan

During the next few years, you may research many jobs. This research can help you make educational plans, so you should keep a record of it. To do this, each time you finish a Career Research Record, fill in the Career Research Summaries in your Individual Career Plan.

You have now completed all the *Pathfinder* activities that helped you make career and educational choices based on your interests and needs. Because those choices are recorded in your Individual Career Plan, you now have a permanent record of the choices you've made so far. Part 6 of *Pathfinder* contains your ICP, and it also includes a section to help you work on high school planning.

Plans for the Future

Keeping Records

This final part of *Pathfinder* doesn't contain more activities. Its purpose is to be a permanent record of the choices you make as you complete the activities in other parts. This record is called your *Individual Career Plan (ICP)*. Your ICP then becomes a useful reference tool for making future plans for high school and beyond. As you make decisions about your future, you can use the information in your ICP for guidance.

This part also includes a section to plan your high school career. This section is a place to begin the planning process—your school also will provide help and guidance for planning your high school schedule both before you start and during your high school years. If you've already started high school, you can use the plan to review courses you've taken and to think about where you want to go. Reviewing data in your ICP can help you make decisions that match your educational and career interests.

Individual Career Plan

Name: _____ Date: _____

Grade: _____ School: _____

✳ Directions

Fill in item 1. Refer back to your Career Interest Groups Record in Part 1 for this information (it starts on page 21).

1. **Career Interest Groups Record:** Write your three highest career interest group choices and the subgroups that interest you in these top three choices.

   First career interest group: _____

   Subgroups that interest me in this group: _____

   _____

   Second career interest group: _____

   Subgroups that interest me in this group: _____

   _____

   Third career interest group: _____

   Subgroups that interest me in this group: _____

   _____

✳ Directions

Record your choices from Part 2 to fill in items 2 through 7.

2. **Data, People, and Things Choices:** Complete the following statements using the answers you wrote in the box on page 44.

   I would most like a career where I work the most with

   _____

I would also not mind working with

_____

I would least like to work with

_____

3. **Work Value Choices:** Complete the following statements using the answers you wrote in the box on page 46.

   My first work value choice is

   _____

   My second work value choice is

   _____

   My third work value choice is

   _____

4. **Work Environment and Conditions Choices:** Complete the following statements using the answers you wrote in the box on page 48.

   Of the three basic choices, Inside, Outside, or Both, I would like a job working

   _____

   I could work in an environment that includes these conditions:

   _____

   _____

   _____

   I do not want to work in an environment that includes these conditions:

   _____

   _____

   _____

   _____

5. **Physical Needs Choices:** Complete the following statement using the answer you wrote in the box on page 49.

I would like a job that does not require me to

_____

_____

_____

6. **Nontraditional Career Choices:** Refer to the box on page 52 to complete the following statement.

The nontraditional careers (if any) that interest me are

_____

_____

_____

_____

7. **Entrepreneurship Choices:** Explain why you would or would not like to run your own business some day on the lines below (refer to the box on page 52).

_____

_____

_____

_____

Directions

Your answers in Part 3 will help you to fill in number 8. Refer to number 1 on the Connecting Academic Achievement to Work Habits and Interpersonal Skills worksheet (see page 69) and the box on page 70.

8. **Goals for Improvement:** Complete the following statements.

I need to improve my work in the following three academic classes:

_____

_____

_____

Achieving these three goals will help me improve my work habits and academic achievement:

_____

_____

_____

Directions

Use the answers you gave in the worksheets in Part 4 to help you complete number 9.

9. **Postsecondary Educational Paths:** Rank your choices for postsecondary education from 1 to 4, with 1 being the path that most interests you. Circle your top two choices.

_____ Technical/Trade   _____ College Prep

_____ Associate Degree   _____ College Prep+

If the technical/trade path was one of your top two choices, what type of technical/trade training interests you? (See number 3 on page 75.) Write your top two choices on the lines below.

_____

_____

If the college prep or college prep+ path was one of your top choices, what majors or areas of study interest you? (See number 2 on page 78.) Write your top two choices on the lines below.

_____

_____

Career Research Summaries

Directions

Follow your Career Research Record to summarize each job you research.

Job Title: _____

Career interest group and subgroup:_____

Core academic skills needed for this job: _____

_____

High school classes recommended for this job, if any: _____

_____

Educational path recommended for this job: _____

Things I like about this job: _____

_____

_____

Things I dislike about this job: _____

_____

_____

Job Title: _____

Career interest group and subgroup: _____

Core academic skills needed for this job: _____

_____

High school classes recommended for this job, if any: _____

_____

Educational path recommended for this job: _____

Things I like about this job: _____

_____

_____

Things I dislike about this job: _____

_____

_____

Job Title: _____

Career interest group and subgroup: _____

Core academic skills needed for this job: _____

_____

High school classes recommended for this job, if any: _____

_____

Educational path recommended for this job: _____

Things I like about this job: _____

_____

_____

Things I dislike about this job: _____

_____

Job Title: _____

Career interest group and subgroup: _____

Core academic skills needed for this job: _____

_____

High school classes recommended for this job, if any: _____

_____

Educational path recommended for this job: _____

Things I like about this job: _____

_____

_____

Things I dislike about this job: _____

_____

_____

Job Title: _____

Career interest group and subgroup: _____

Core academic skills needed for this job: _____

_____

High school classes recommended for this job, if any: _____

_____

Educational path recommended for this job: _____

Things I like about this job: _____

_____

_____

Things I dislike about this job: _____

_____

_____

High School Planning

Because you may just be starting high school, you might wonder why *Pathfinder* focuses on the many educational options open to you after high school! You might think, "What's the rush?" Hopefully, the activities in *Pathfinder* have shown you that your schoolwork now and in high school is very closely linked to your career and educational choices in the future.

As you progress through high school, you should think about whether you prefer to focus on work immediately after high school. You might go directly into a job or the military or get postsecondary training that teaches you job-related skills for a specific career. If one of these is your choice, then you want to take as many courses as you can in high school that will prepare you for the work at a particular job or in a particular career area. Remember, all jobs require proficiency in the core academic skills, too. Make sure your high school plan covers both. When you share your career interest with your teachers and counselors, they will help you find courses your high school offers to guide you. Then you'll be ready to perform well in the technical/trade path you select after high school.

If you want to earn a two-year associate degree or a four-year bachelor's degree after high school, you should take a college prep path in high school. Schooling for an associate degree or a bachelor's degree both include taking advanced core academic subjects and classes to learn job-related skills for a specific career or a career area. A college prep path will prepare you for this level of work. If your high school offers courses in a career area that interests you, you can take those as electives.

Reviewing the career research you've done and doing more career research can help you make a plan for high school. If a particular career really interests you, you need to know the education it requires. Reviewing your interests and plans each year will prepare you for any future choice or challenges. Good luck!

High School Course Selection

You will need the help of your teacher, school counselor, and parent(s) or guardian(s) to select your high school course of study. Your choices will be controlled, of course, by the classes your high school offers. Not all schools offer the same programs. This is especially true of vocational preparation classes. To begin planning, you'll need to know all the classes currently available at the high school you will attend.

Although the following planner contains sections to plan all four years of high school, remember this plan is just the beginning. You may want to plan only your first two years now. You may plan all four years now. You may already be in high school and have completed some high school work. However, after you complete each year of high school, you should review your past classes and your plans for the next year to see whether you want to make any changes. Hopefully, you will have completed more career research, and those new insights will help you make revisions if you need them. Thinking about postsecondary educational paths you like and your career interests will help you to shape your plans.

Directions

Complete the High School Planner by following these steps:

1. Fill out the required courses section for each year. Your school will have a list of these. If you don't know which educational path you want to take—technical/trade, associate degree, or college preparatory—select courses for your first two years that will keep all paths open.

2. Select elective courses. You might pick ones that will prepare you for the educational path you like or ones that match a career interest. Electives are great for picking something that just sounds interesting or different. Your elective classes can open new interests.

3. Consider extracurricular activities. Vocational clubs and other activities might relate to a career you like. For example, if you are interested in teaching or law, the debate team would improve your reasoning and language skills. Clubs are also usually available in subject areas such as foreign language or drama. You may pick an activity because you enjoy it. Sports teams or music groups are good examples. The high school you plan to attend should have a list of available extracurricular activities. The more involved you are in your high school, the more likely you are to enjoy your high school years. Thinking about extracurricular activities beforehand is a good way to get involved.

4. Write in any outside activities. These could include hobbies, volunteer or part-time jobs, summer jobs, or family responsibilities. Think about how these activities could help you develop the work habits and interpersonal skills you need at school and on the job and write down the ideas you have.

High School Planner

Grade 9

	Required Courses	Elective Courses
First Semester:	_____	_____
	_____	_____
	_____	_____
	_____	_____
	_____	_____
	_____	_____
Second Semester:	_____	_____
	_____	_____
	_____	_____
	_____	_____
	_____	_____

Extracurricular Activities:

_____

_____

_____

Outside Activities:

_____

_____

_____

Grade 10

	Required Courses	Elective Courses
First Semester:	_____	_____
	_____	_____
	_____	_____
	_____	_____
	_____	_____
	_____	_____
Second Semester:	_____	_____
	_____	_____
	_____	_____
	_____	_____
	_____	_____

Extracurricular Activities:

_____

_____

_____

Outside Activities:

_____

_____

_____

Grade 11

Required Courses	Elective Courses

First Semester:

_____   _____

_____   _____

_____   _____

_____   _____

_____   _____

_____   _____

Second Semester:

_____   _____

_____   _____

_____   _____

_____   _____

_____   _____

_____   _____

Extracurricular Activities:

_____

_____

_____

Outside Activities:

_____

_____

_____

Grade 12

	Required Courses	Elective Courses
First Semester:	_____	_____
	_____	_____
	_____	_____
	_____	_____
	_____	_____
Second Semester:	_____	_____
	_____	_____
	_____	_____
	_____	_____
	_____	_____

Extracurricular Activities:

_____

_____

_____

Outside Activities:

_____

_____